1992. Happy Birthday -
Donna

D0443381

That Ye May Believe

That Ye May Believe

Neal A. Maxwell

I write unto you . . . that ye may believe
—Mormon 3:20–21

BOOKCRAFT
Salt Lake City, Utah

Library of Congress Catalog Card Number: 92-72664

ISBN 0–88494–843–9

First Printing, 1992

Printed in the United States of America

To Colleen's and my grandchildren:

Erik Ahlander	Ryan Anderson
Andrea Ahlander	Brittany Anderson
Robbie Ahlander	Lindsey Anderson
	Michael Anderson
Peter Maxwell	Katie Anderson
Emily Maxwell	
Brian Maxwell	Heather Sanders
Elizabeth Maxwell	Ashley Sanders
Sarah Jane Maxwell	Kimball Sanders
Martha Maxwell	Jacob Sanders
Timothy Maxwell	Lauren Sanders

Thanks for brightening and enriching our lives on this side of the veil. While hoping our time with you here will stretch for a few more seasons, nevertheless we look forward to everlasting life with each and all of you.

These letters are offered in supplementation of our efforts during the periodic firesides for the grandchildren. Selfishly, we enjoy being with you so much and especially the gospel conversations we share.

Gratefully, we remember your signed pledge given on our fortieth wedding anniversary: "We will do our best to ensure there will be no empty chairs when we meet in the life beyond." In turn, we will do our best to endure to the end and to prepare those chairs for you!

Contents

Preface

This book consists of letters written to our grandchildren *as if* they were older. Though these involve *imaginary* inquiries, they certainly do not involve imaginary concerns, hence my commentaries are real. These grandchildren will likely ponder these and other concerns in their mature years or as young parents. Therefore, while my answers do not now intersect with their present capacity to so ask questions, it seemed desirable to attempt a blend of anticipation, affection, and counsel.

Fortunately, all these grandchildren have loving, special, and spiritually informed parents to nurture them. Even so, my counsel is proffered prospectively and affectionately, for "such as I have, give I" unto them.

The words of loving counsel and encouragement are offered—*as if* we were corresponding and conversing—as a small storehouse for use in their seasons of soul stretching.

Along with the scriptures, likewise included are quotations from the early Brethren found primarily in the *Journal of Discourses*, a source most readers may understandably not explore, so my eyes have done the scanning in a search for words of special relevance for our time. Most frequently, the quotations are from President Brigham Young who, too often, is thought of as primarily a colonizer, a pioneer leader. In fact, he is also a major source of doctrine and deserves far more attention than he often receives for his treasure trove of teachings, many relayed from the Prophet Joseph Smith but still others from his own insights and revelations.

C. S. Lewis is quoted here from time to time, not for his theology but for his phraseology. His articulation reflects his religious resolution and is such that all may profit thereby.

George MacDonald was Lewis's mentor *in absentia*. The connections are clear, but MacDonald is very articulate in his own right, as samples will show.

Acknowledgments

This book is not an official Church publication. I alone am responsible for its contents.

I am indebted to three friends for reacting to early drafts of this book. One of them, Roy W. Doxey, though ill with cancer, has been kind enough to review manuscripts for me several times before. His illness may mean that this is the last time; thus I thank Roy doubly for his service, and, most of all, salute him for a life of service in the kingdom.

Two very busy and very effective friends, James S. Jardine and H. E. "Bud" Scruggs, Jr., have been especially helpful, not only in reacting to the format but also with various other suggestions. I am indebted to them for this service.

Susan Jackson, once more, has been patient in processing these words through several drafts. So helpful in so many ways, Susan has my deep appreciation.

To all my friends at Bookcraft, especially George Bickerstaff and Cory Maxwell, I extend my appreciation for their patient editing and for encouraging this project.

Submission to God's Will

Dear Brian:

When we last visited, you mentioned Jesus' special, post-atonement words "and would that I might not . . . shrink." These are especially precious and disclosing. Moreover, these words are found in only one place in all of holy writ (D&C 19:18). Since these words describe Jesus' profound, personal feelings while accomplishing the great atonement, they are uniquely worth pondering.

To "shrink" means to "recoil," to "draw back," even to "cower." During the Atonement—awful and agonizing beyond our capacity to comprehend—the possibility existed that, if not fully submissive, Jesus could "draw back." He did not have to die! Thus, He voluntarily experienced "the fierceness of the wrath of Almighty God" (D&C 76:107; see also 88:106). Severe, divine justice was administered—because God "cannot look upon sin with the least degree of allowance"—which worked its will upon Jesus as He bore all human sins, including those of the "vilest of sinners" (see D&C 1:31; Mosiah 28:4).

Additional agony was imposed, according to President Brigham Young:

> God never bestows upon His people, or upon an individual, superior blessings without a severe trial to prove them, . . . Then the greater the vision, the greater the display of the power of the enemy. . . . For this express purpose the Father withdrew His spirit from His Son, at the time he was to be crucified. Jesus had been with his Father, talked with Him, dwelt in His bosom, and knew all about heaven, about making the earth, about the transgression of man, and what would redeem the people, and that he was the character who was to redeem the sons of

earth, and the earth itself from all sin that had come upon it. The light, knowledge, power, and glory with which he was clothed were far above, or exceeded that of all others who had been upon the earth after the fall, consequently at the very moment, at the hour when the crisis came for him to offer up his life, the Father withdrew Himself, withdrew His Spirit, and cast a veil over him. That is what made him sweat blood. If he had had the power of God upon him, he would not have sweat blood; but all was withdrawn from him, and a veil was cast over him, and he then plead with the Father not to forsake him.[1]

Hence Jesus was in the position of treading the winepress totally "alone." Truly "there was none with [Him]." (Isaiah 63:3; see also D&C 76:107; 88:106; 133:50.)

It was all made possible by the Savior's splendid submissiveness. He did voluntarily what He was not forced to do; it was something no other child of God could do! "There was no other good enough to pay the price of sin" (*Hymns* no. 194). "Yea, even so he shall be led, crucified, and slain, the flesh becoming subject even unto death, the will of the Son being swallowed up in the will of the Father" (Mosiah 15:7). The imagery and theology of this verse tell us that Jesus was totally, perfectly, and fully consecrated.

Being "swallowed up" means being totally enveloped— without question, protest, reservation, or resentment. It is "all the way," not halfway. Choosing such spiritual submission is the highest act of deliberate, individual will: "And he said, Abba, Father, all things are possible unto thee; take away this cup from me: *nevertheless* not what I will, but what thou wilt" (Mark 14:36; emphasis added).

Though Jesus' will was thus "swallowed up," we certainly don't notice any diminution of Jesus' individuality after the Atonement, do we? In fact, not only was He resplendent, but after the Resurrection, amid some of His sheep, He declared that His joy was now "full" (3 Nephi 17:20). Consecration enhances individuality. Furthermore, when we are "swallowed up" in His will we will also know what it is like to be "swallowed up in the joy of Christ" (Alma 31:38).

Thereafter meek Christ also included himself, along with the Father, as model and exemplar for us (see 3 Nephi 12:48; 27:27). The glory He had with the Father before the world was, immense beyond our imagination, was "added upon" (see John 17:5, 24; Abraham 3:26).

Included in Jesus' enhancement was extraordinary, even unique, empathy, now fully like His Father's. Elder George Q. Cannon explained:

> He has watched over us tenderly and kindly, giving us a blessing here and a blessing there, a revelation here and a revelation there, a precept here and a precept there, as we could bear them, developing our experience, and knowledge, and our wisdom, leading us gently and safely in the path that will bring us into his presence. . . .
>
> He knows how to guide us and how to time his blessings to our wants; and when you feel impatient and dissatisfied because he does not give you more than you now have, and when you are afflicted and bowed down in sorrow and pain, let the reflection enter into your hearts to comfort you, that our Father and God, our Lord and Savior Jesus Christ, trod the path we are now treading, that there is no affliction and sorrow that we are acquainted with, or can be, that the Lord has not already had an experience in; and he knows our condition, he knows what is good for us. If we need a gift and a blessing, he knows when to bestow it upon us.[2]

For us on our small scale, submission includes not shrinking, either, not drawing back from what is presented to us to cope with in our lives. We see this in President Brigham Young's life, which is one reason to quote from him often. As he said, even in the midst of deep and discouraging blackness we are to trust in the Lord in order to show that we are "a friend of God" by being "righteous in the dark."[3] On another occasion, Brigham Young called for us to be faithful even if circumstances are "darker than 10,000 midnights."[4] Some of us murmur even when only the dusk of difficulty appears.

One example of Brigham Young's observing without complaining is that he had been driven from his home five times, leaving behind everything he had.[5] Upon returning from one mission, though in impoverished circumstances, yet he was submissive.

> I returned again in two years, and found that I had spent hundreds of dollars, which I had accumulated on my mission, to help the brethren to emigrate to Nauvoo, and had but one sovereign left. I said I would buy a barrel of flour with that, and sit down and eat it with my wife and children, and I determined I would not ask anybody for work, until I had eaten it all up. Brother Joseph asked me how I intended to live. I said, "I will go to work and get a living." I tarried in Nauvoo from the year 1841 to 1846, the year we left. In that time I had accumulated much property, for the Lord multiplied everything in my hands, and blessed all my undertakings. But I never ceased to preach; and travelled every season, both in the winter, and in the summer. I was at home occasionally, and the Lord fed and clothed me. It has never entered into my heart, from the first day I was called to preach the Gospel to this day, when the Lord said, "Go and leave your family," to offer the least objection.[6]

Our personal possessions and our material blessings are really not ours, so what we sometimes regard as a sacrifice was given to us, anyway. President Young understood this: "How long have we got to live before we find out that we have nothing to consecrate to the Lord—that all belongs to the Father in heaven; that these mountains are His; the valleys, the timber, the water, the soil; in fine, the earth and its fulness?"[7]

A degree of developmental difficulty we experience will precede any "superior blessings" we receive, just as President Young likewise declared. Furthermore, President John Taylor noted several times that Joseph Smith told the Twelve the Lord would even "wrench" their very heartstrings.[8] However, it is vital to know Whose hand is doing the wrenching.

If, however, we yield to the will of God, we are carried along by spiritual surf to higher realms, ranging far beyond that which we could attain by ourselves. Besides, as to trials, Jesus asked searchingly whether the servant is above his master (see Matthew 10:24).

So it is that we cannot expect to be strangers to suffering. Peter candidly counseled accordingly: "Beloved, think it not strange concerning the fiery trial which is to try you, as though some strange thing happened unto you. . . . Yet if any man suffer as a Christian, let him not be ashamed; but let him glorify God on this behalf. . . . Wherefore let them that suffer according to the will of God commit the keeping of their souls to him in well doing, as unto a faithful Creator." (1 Peter 4:12, 16, 19.)

Jesus' disciples are no strangers to that dimension of suffering involving aloneness. This challenge may come at different and unpredictable times for almost all of us and may include experience with loneliness. It did for Moroni: "Behold, my father hath made this record, and he hath written the intent thereof. And behold, I would write it also if I had room upon the plates, but I have not; and ore I have none, for I am alone. My father hath been slain in battle, and all my kinsfolk, and I have not friends nor whither to go; and how long the Lord will suffer that I may live I know not." (Mormon 8:5.)

You have endured some visual deprivation, yet the important things you have seen so clearly.

Eternal love,
Grandpa Neal

Notes

1. *Journal of Discourses* 3:205–6. (Hereafter cited as *JD*.)
2. *JD* 11:174–75.
3. Brigham Young's Office Journal, 28 January 1857.
4. *JD* 3:207.

5. *JD* 7:205.
6. *JD* 2:19. See also *JD* 7:230.
7. *JD* 2:308.
8. *JD* 24:197.

Keep Checking the Fig Tree

Dear Martha:

How much time before the Second Coming? Since the angels, otherwise well-informed individuals, do not know the day or the hour (how about the year?), certainly none of us does. Even so, though we are deprived of precision, we can still observe the leaves on the fig tree and the prophesied signs of the times. On the one hand, clearly there is so much which is yet to come to pass: first, the gospel shall be preached to every nation for a witness (see Matthew 24:14). But on the other hand, many events can be compressed into a short space of time (for instance, the opening of doors to nations that are now shut).

In recent years we have witnessed world events which nearly all experts thought would take decades to evolve. Moreover, the Lord has promised to hasten His work in its time (see D&C 88:73).

Additionally there is also Jesus' promise that "for the elect's sake" the last days would be shortened (Matthew 24:22). Apparently, severe conditions will take such a toll that this hastening and shortening will be necessary and merciful.

Do take time to smell the flowers, but occasionally check the leaves on the fig tree to see if summer is nigh!

Eternal love,
Grandfather

The Ninth Commandment

Dear Andrea:

The ninth commandment is neglected, being seldom discussed at any length. There are so many different ways to breach "Thou shalt not bear false witness against thy neighbor" (Exodus 20:16). We can spread falsehood knowingly and maliciously rather than inadvertently. Perhaps that is the worst form of breaking this commandment. We can also spread falsehood by simply passing it along in the form of idle gossip without malicious intent, which is somewhat mitigating.

Either way, the innocent victim usually experiences a double blow: first, damage to his self-image/self-confidence; second, the diminished regard of others. Additionally, the victim probably comes to have diminished regard, even anger, toward those who so traffic in untruth.

The key to understanding this commandment is to be found in the two words *false witness*. What is communicated is "false"; it violates the truth. The adding thereto of one's own "witness" is a harmful violation of integrity. Bearing false witness not only hurts the victim; in addition others are misled thereby, basing their decisions, opinions, and attitudes on false information—"I seem to remember something that . . ."

Worse still, false accusations can linger like a bad odor. The victim may even be vindicated without being re-established. He may be exonerated but remain excluded.

Wilford Woodruff observed: "To me the principle of integrity is one of the greatest blessings we can possibly possess. He who proves true to himself or his brethren, to his friends and his God, will have the evidence within him that he is accepted; he will have the confidence of his God and of his friends."[1] Sustained integrity does become its own true witness! You will recall the Lord's saying that He loved

Hyrum Smith for "the integrity of his heart" (D&C 124:15).

Some engage in character assassination in a most unusual way. They attack, libel, and defame in such a way as to require the accused individuals to prove a negative, a very difficult thing to do. Moreover, sometimes wild assertions are such that the response of suffering in silence will not do; they demand a response, which may be scrutinized more than the accusations!

Denials, likewise, seldom overtake all the charges. Even legitimate concerns, when wrapped inside hysteria or swollen by frequent repetition, are difficult to handle.

As with all of the commandments, the breaching of the ninth commandment reflects a fundamental lack of love of God and of His children, our neighbors. True love never lies; it is not even eager to believe the worst about someone. Most of us, though essentially decent, need to work on achieving higher levels of integrity, if only by improving the nuances of our communications. Our tongue is part of the problem, for in its use we frequently tell more about ourselves than about those we diminish: "When a person opens his mouth, no matter what he talks about, to a person of quick discernment, he will disclose more or less of his true sentiments. You cannot hide the heart, when the mouth is open. . . . If you let your tongue run, and it scatters the poison that is in you, it sets the whole being on fire."[2]

No wonder James warned that one's religion was vain if he could not bridle his tongue (see James 1:26; 3:5-6).

I love you.
Grandfather

Notes

1. JD 8:266.
2. Brigham Young, *JD* 6:74.

The Plan We Approved

Dear Ashley:

You inquired about life's demanding structure and the sometimes turbulent flow of things. Such cause us to ponder, don't they?

If God were to set up a world in which we would have no memories of our first estate; in which our faith and patience would be deliberately and regularly tried; in which we would be daily proved; in which we would walk by faith, not by sight; in which we would be individually tutored; in which we would be asked to endure well, while accepting that God loves us, even when we cannot always understand the meaning of all things—if He set up such a world, wouldn't living in it be just about what we experience now?

If we criticize God or are unduly miffed over sufferings and tribulation, we are really criticizing the Planner for implementing the very plan we once approved, premortally (see Job 38:4, 7). Granted, we don't now remember the actual approval. But not remembering is actually part of the plan!

In the midst of vexing difficulties, since we shouted "for joy" in the premortal world, sometimes we may wonder now what all the shouting was about! However, our justified shouting for joy occurred in another place, in another time, and with another perspective. In our second estate we lack the memories of our first estate. We walk by faith here in the "muddled middle"—bereft of premortal memories. There—prospectively, at least—we saw the end from the beginning.

In the muddled middle it is easy for some to decry the human circumstance or even to scoff at their Benefactor.

Thanks for being "anxiously engaged" and for playing upon my heartstrings as you have played so beautifully on your violin strings!

Eternal love,
Grandfather

Longsuffering

Dear Peter:

Ah, yes, learning to cope with disappointment in others. It's almost as grating and hard to bear as disappointment with oneself.

The poignancy of your disappointment over your friend's situation underscores how much all of us need to develop further our own capacity to be *longsuffering*. Jesus is so longsuffering with us!

Longsuffering involves not only bearing our own trials and disappointments but also behaving patiently, empathetically, and redemptively toward others. In the spiritual scheme of things, the lubricant of longsuffering is vital. My willingness to try to do better, for instance, can be cut short by the discouraging expression of another's sharp impatience. Yet we seldom speak of this unglamorous virtue; perhaps we mistakenly confuse longsuffering with indifference or indulgence. Obviously there is suffering in longsuffering, including deep and repeated disappointment. But longsuffering does not give up easily.

Consumed by his selfishness, the natural man is anything but longsuffering. He is reflexively insensitive to and impatient with others, including those in his own family. Even when we are under way in the development of longsuffering, it is a long way from first noticing the needs of others to going on to exhibit real forgiving and longsuffering.

As with all of the eternal virtues, the family garden is the best place in which to grow and nurture the capacity for longsuffering. Daily family life is filled with opportunities to extend love and mercy. Building a tradition of meekness in which such spiritual transactions are emotionally inexpensive is such a blessing. The less pride, the less pouting. Qualities which do not sprout in that nutritive garden have a much harder time in the more arid climates and the thinner soil of the business, political, or academic worlds.

You put it adroitly: "It is better to put up with someone than to put him down." Still better, however, is lifting someone up! Sometimes we must do more than reach out gesturingly: with longsuffering we actually search for others' hands, because some have been disappointed so many times that their hands no longer even reach out for help. These are the "hands which hang down" (Hebrews 12:12).

Obviously, the same things could be said of longsuffering's sister quality of *patience*, which is especially needed since, rather than our being able to rush matters, "all things must come to pass in their time" (D&C 64:32). God's timetable—not ours—will prevail. Therefore, our capacity for waiting becomes vital. Certain pivotal things happen not only in "God's own time" but also "in his own way, and according to his own will" (D&C 88:68; see also 136:18; 2 Nephi 27:21; 1 Peter 5:6).

Obedience and longsuffering are also symbiotic, for we exist in a universe of law wherein God's work is extensively under way. Without obedience to Him it is not safe for us to share His power. In fact, the powers of heaven simply cannot be controlled except "upon the principles of righteousness" (D&C 121:36). Mercifully it is so. Unlike the situation in the mercurial mortal scene, heavenly thrones and powers are never in danger of the coup or the takeover.

Ahead in eternity there may be "narrow passages" yet to be navigated, passages which are unknown to us now. Strict obedience will still be essential. Otherwise we would not really be equipped to live in such a universe, which, for all we know, will require not only our obedience but also spiritual daring in order for us to come safely through.

Obedience to the requirements of spiritual sacrifice is actually an opportunity. Said Brigham Young:

> Time and time again have I left handsome property to be inherited by our enemies.
> Suppose we were called to leave what we have now, should we call it a sacrifice? Shame on the man who

would so call it; for it is the very means of adding to him knowledge, understanding, power, and glory, and prepares him to receive crowns, kingdoms, thrones, and principalities, and to be crowned in glory with the Gods of eternity. Short of this, we can never receive that which we are looking for.[1]

Then instead of concluding that the Lord has drawn us into difficulties, and compelled us to do that which is unpleasant to our feelings, and to suffer sacrifice upon sacrifice to no purpose, we shall understand that He has designed all this to prepare us to dwell in His presence, to possess His Spirit, which is right and intelligent, for nothing but purity and holiness can dwell where He is. He has so ordained it, that by the natural mind we cannot see and understand the things of God, therefore we must then seek unto the Lord, and get His Spirit and the light thereof, to understand His will. And when He is calling us to pass through that which we call afflictions, trials, temptations, and difficulties, did we possess the light of the Spirit, we would consider this the greatest blessing that could be bestowed upon us.[2]

Easy as it is to say and hard as it is to do, some of our unwanted and unscheduled spiritual "workouts" should thus be viewed differently, by using the eyes of faith, which help us to be longsuffering.

It is a spiritual fact that there can be no self-improvement without challenges to self. Understandably, we may wish it were otherwise. A particular challenge to our longsuffering may be either direct or subtle, brief or prolonged. Whichever, the status quo may even need to be shaken "for thy good" and to "give thee experience" (D&C 122:7). We don't like such shakings any more than we like the unnerving tremors of earthquakes, do we? We are not expected to like it, but we are expected to endure it.

In any case, becoming more like Christ "here and now" will also help us do His work better in the later "there and then." By the way, most of the work we do in the spirit world will be done among those millions who never really heard of Christ during their mortal lives. Awesome differences in mortal cultures and experiences will need to be lovingly confronted there. The justice and mercy of God require that each individual be given a real chance to hear the gospel fully. True disciples are "ready always" to contribute articulately to God's work at any time and in any place (1 Peter 3:15). All will then be permitted to choose personally and irrevocably, before the final judgment.

Can we expect to help effectively as messengers in God's vast work—whether there or here—unless we become more longsuffering like Him whose great message we bear?

Furthermore, longsuffering facilitates the shedding of our selfishness. This is a large and difficult part of putting off the natural man, a necessary act before re-entry to Father's house. Only then can we be fully "at home" with Him, comfortable and confident in His presence (D&C 121:45).

Thanks for being a pathfinder. Brothers, sisters, and cousins will notice your footprints. Make those marks meekly and carefully.

Eternal love,
Grandfather

Notes

1. JD 2:7.
2. JD 2:303.

Democracy, Equality, Fulness

Dear Timothy:

You are quite right: parents at times are not very democratic! A true story from the Oscar W. McConkie, Sr., family speaks to this issue. One of the children complained to the father on a Sunday afternoon, saying, "Dad, I don't have to go to sacrament meeting if I don't want to, do I?" To which Oscar W. McConkie, Sr., replied, "Of course you don't! Now hurry and get your coat, or we'll be late for sacrament meeting!" It is in the very nature of parenting that parents need to be authoritative, yet without being authoritarian.

Our respect for democratic procedures should not obscure the reality that power resides somewhere—even in the mob—and it often shows itself in interesting ways. George Will describes how authority can operate even in supposedly democratic university settings. Benjamin Jowett was once the head of one of Oxford's colleges: "Once when Jowett submitted a matter to a vote of Balliol's dons and was displeased with the results, he announced, 'The vote is 22-to-2. I see we are deadlocked.' "[1]

The requirements of the gospel are deeply democratic. All are to walk the same straight and narrow path. All are to keep the same commandments and covenants. But what will result is an eventual aristocracy of Saints. It will be the only safe, deserving, and righteous aristocracy in all of history!

Additionally, according to Brigham Young, while we will receive a fulness of God's blessings, "every one will be rewarded and enjoy according to his capacity. Each vessel will be filled to overflowing, and hence all will be equal, in that they are full. Every man and woman will receive to a fulness, though the quantity will vary according to the extent of their capacity, and each will be crowned with glory and eternal life, if faithful."[2]

Thus there will be equality in that each of the faithful receives "to a fulness."

How, you may ask, does this square with the scriptures which tell us that the fully faithful will receive "all that my Father hath"? (D&C 84:38.) "All" is "all," isn't it? Ponder this verse: "Whatever principle of intelligence we attain unto in this life, it will rise with us in the resurrection. And if a person gains more knowledge and intelligence in this life through his diligence and obedience than another, he will have *so much the advantage in the world to come.* (D&C 130:19, emphasis added.)

And this verse too: "Howbeit that he made the greater star; as, also, if there be two spirits, and one shall be more intelligent than the other, yet these two spirits, notwithstanding one is more intelligent than the other, have no beginning; they existed before, they shall have no end, they shall exist after, for they are gnolaum, or eternal" (Abraham 3:18).

There will thus be individual differences but amid individual fulness! Besides, the glories that await are presently unimaginable to our mortal minds, exceeding our fondest expectations.

Our crimped and cramped perspective, which goes with the mortal territory, keeps us from seeing certain things clearly. The veil blocks out memories of the first estate and views of the third, unless the Lord, under certain special conditions, chooses to reveal these to us.

Be patient with your parents, as they have been with you!

I love you.
Grandfather

Notes

1. *The American Scholar*, Autumn 1991, p. 502.
2. JD 7:7.

Putting Off the Natural Man

Dear Kimball:

We sometimes use shorthand in our communications, casually assuming others will understand. Apparently I have done that in our firesides by merely referencing the "natural man." So here is a little elaboration.

Behold the natural man! Selfish, impatient, short-tempered, easily offended, unforgiving, proud, envious, covetous, carnal, and drenched in ego! No wonder he is to be "put off." (Mosiah 3:19; Colossians 3:8; Romans 6:6; Ephesians 4:22.) Nevertheless, he is very difficult to put off. The old ways, so pleasing to the carnal man, are really hard to set aside. Actually, these ways are not really fulfilling and not really satisfying. But they are preoccupying, for pleasing the natural man is a full-time business. He sees to that!

Paul and King Benjamin agree that we are to put off the old man, or the natural man (Mosiah 3:19; Colossians 3:9–10). Whereas Paul would have us put on the new man, King Benjamin describes the process as that of becoming a saint. Elsewhere the process is described as becoming the "man of Christ" (Helaman 3:29). In any case, we seek to have the "mind of Christ" and to strive to become "even as [He] is" (1 Corinthians 2:16; 3 Nephi 27:27).

Of course, what is really to be jettisoned, put off, is anger, selfishness, malice, injustice, impatience, filthy communication, and so forth, while we put on kindness, meekness, longsuffering, and so on (see Colossians 3:9–10).

Not only is the natural man heavy to carry but his eyes are congenitally flawed; he obscures our view of the things which matter most, which "are spiritually discerned" (1 Corinthians 2:14).

Thanks for your spiritual alertness. I love you.

Grandfather

Eternal, Intelligent, Independent

Dear Jacob:

Brigham Young spoke several times of that intrinsic independence which each person has, which is to be further developed and tried in the process of life. "When God organized intelligent beings, he organized them as independent beings to a certain extent, as he is himself. And whether we see an evil act or a good one performed by an intelligent being, that being has performed the act by his will, by his own independent organization, which is capable of doing good or evil."[1] And again, "The will I am speaking about is implanted in us by him; and the spirit of every intelligent being is organized to become independent according to its capacity."[2]

Whatever that eternal element the spirit consists of, according to Brigham Young it is independent. The revelations likewise imply (see D&C 93:29; Abraham 3:18).

The doctrine of premortality declares that, before his mortal birth, "man was also in the beginning with God" (D&C 93:29). Therefore you have been you for a long, long time. Furthermore, though some important details are as yet unrevealed, certain spirit elements of man "are eternal" and "have no beginning," since "intelligence, or the light of truth, was not created or made, neither indeed can be" (D&C 93:29–33). Joseph Smith added, "It existed from eternity and will exist to eternity."[3]

President Joseph Fielding Smith observed: "We have never been given any insight into this matter beyond what the Lord has fragmentarily revealed. We know, however, that there is something called intelligence which always existed. It is the real eternal part of man, which was not created or made. This intelligence combined with the spirit constitutes a spiritual identity or individual."[4]

Whatever that unique dimension of spirit or self is, it preceded what Heavenly Father did in the creation of us as His spirit sons and daughters. In that sense, God may be operating within whatever parameters preceded our spiritual creation. His cumulative loving-kindnesses made it all possible!

We should focus more on our possibilities than our independencies, however, for, said Brigham Young, "man possesses the germ of all the attributes and power that are possessed by God. . . . that God possesses in perfection."[5]

Brigham Young observed too that, of all the things upon which Latter-day Saints should concentrate, though we are independent beings, it should be to develop our love or charity.[6] He further observed that it is out of love that the other virtues proceed, such as patience, longsuffering, kindness, and forgiveness. Of course, President Young was just simply underscoring what the Savior said about the two great commandments being preeminent—upon these "hang all the law and the prophets" (Matthew 22:40). Moreover, he counseled, "sin is . . . an inversion of the attributes God has placed in [man]."[7]

Every edifying quality or attribute, at the initiating point, arises from and depends upon love. Therefore our capacity to love determines the extent to which we can be patient, meek, forgiving, and kind. This is an especially important consideration, when we think that in the last days the love of many will wax cold; it will not merely become lukewarm or cool (see Matthew 24:12).

Paul urged us to seek the "mind of Christ" (1 Corinthians 2:16), but we should also seek the heart of Christ. Significantly, in the unparalleled city of Enoch, the inhabitants were of "one heart and one mind" (see Moses 7:18).

We read in the Gospel of John the Savior's words that "the Son can do nothing of himself, but what he seeth the Father do: for what things soever he doeth, these also doeth the Son likewise" (John 5:19). The Son, who was a perfect pupil, saw His perfect Father exhibit, premortally and otherwise, perfect loving-kindness. Jesus, who so lived himself, beckons us: "What manner of men [and women] ought ye to be? Verily I say unto you, even as I am." (3 Nephi 27:27.)

Chief among all His attributes which we are to emulate is His loving-kindness!

Thanks for your loving-kindness.

Eternal love,
Grandfather

P.S.

One important dimension of loving-kindness is forgiveness. Our generosity, forgetfulness, and forgiveness can often be the equivalent of an "emancipation proclamation" for someone who has erred, as "with the breath of kindness," we "blow the chaff away."

Instead, sometimes we hold people hostage for an old error. Yet we should follow the divine lead, for the Lord has said He will "not mention" our past mistakes if we turn to Him (see Ezekiel 18:22).

Letting an old error go unmentioned may permit someone to be freed of the past he has long since forsaken, by our helping him to no longer feel forsaken!

Notes

1. *JD* 6:146.

2. *JD* 6:332.

3. Joseph Fielding Smith, comp., *Teachings of the Prophet Joseph Smith* (Salt Lake City: Deseret Book Company, 1976), p. 158. (Hereafter cited as *Teachings*.)

4. Joseph Fielding Smith, *The Progress of Man* (Salt Lake City: Genealogical Society, 1936), p. 10.

5. *JD* 10:251.

6. See *JD* 7:133–34.

7. *JD* 10:251.

Life in the Last Days

Dear Lindsey:

You are to live out your life in that prophesied time when "all things shall be in commotion" (D&C 88:91; 45:26). This will be more than geophysical commotion, though there will surely be some of that (D&C 87:6; 88:89). The general topsy-turviness, however, will be even more challenging. Isaiah foretold that values will be inverted: evil will be called good, and good evil (see Isaiah 5:20). Men's hearts shall fail them amid pervasive uncertainty, as the nations of the earth shall be in perplexity with distress (see Luke 21:25).

Living in a time when all things are in commotion will require the faithful to be better prepared than ever, if they are to be regularly and effectively nurtured. People are best nurtured by the Spirit, parents, living prophets, scriptures, and friends. Again, given the litany of prophecy that will be fulfilled in your time, those of us who seek to communicate with your generation may feel much as did Mormon. In writing to his son Moroni about the gross wickedness of the Nephites, Mormon did not want those things to weigh Moroni down (see Moroni 9:25).

Yet dare we ignore prophecy, such as, for instance, those lines which say a devastating scourge or sickness will cover the face of the land? (See D&C 5:19; 45:31.)

Ever be aware that Heavenly Father really "is able to do [His] own work" (2 Nephi 27:21). He has carefully made "ample provision," [1] even amid human wickedness, so that His plans will prevail finally. Long ago He determined that you and other valiant ones would be able to meet the unusual configuration of challenges in your time, provided you are meek and properly prepared. Even so, do not be surprised if from time to time there are individualized injections of irony. Elder George A. Smith taught, "If there is any one thing that is calculated to try us more than another, that thing we may expect to encounter."[2]

I love you.
Grandfather

_____

Notes

1. *Teachings*, p. 220.
2. *JD* 10:68.

Confessing His Hand

Dear Emily:

I was pleased to have you ask about Doctrine and Covenants 59:21, which advises us that the Lord's wrath is especially kindled when, disobediently and unappreciatively, we do not confess His hand in all things. You are exploring this verse a lot sooner than most, frankly. By the way, your Grandmother Colleen was "on to" this particular scripture well before I started the necessary pondering. Some verses do not have the immediate glitter of other nuggets, yet they contain much hidden treasure. This verse is one of those.

We tend to keep certain doctrines and truths at arm's length, including those we most need to embrace! Your asking also indicates you are *searching* and not just *reading* the scriptures. Searching is more than discovering and finding. It is relating the scriptures to each other; it is also assaying, weighing, and analyzing the parts.

Brace yourself, therefore, for a long letter about a short verse, telling more than you perhaps now want to know.

What is it that kindles such special divine displeasure? Ingratitude, to be sure, but surely our meek and perfect Lord is not asking for mere ritual acknowledgment or for superficial praise of the tongue. Instead, we are told about our loving Father, "In all thy ways acknowledge him, and he shall direct thy paths" (Proverbs 3:6).

In addition to *acknowledging* Him by obeying Him, *confessing* His hand means to *avow*. For instance, confessing God's hand in all things includes acknowledging that His accomplishments are witnessed pervasively, since "all things are created and made to bear record of [God]" (Moses 6:63; see also Helaman 8:24).

Truly, for those who have eyes to see, we live in a witnessing world. God's wondrous creations and works testify of their generous creator in so many ways. "The fulness of the earth is yours . . . All [these] things [are] made for the benefit and the use of man. . . . And it pleaseth God that he has given all these things unto man." (D&C 59:16–20.)

We also see His hand in the careful, gradual unfolding of His kingdom in the latter days. President Joseph F. Smith expressed this in this way:

> The hand of the Lord may not be visible to all. There may be many who cannot discern the workings of God's will in the progress and development of this great latter-day work, but there are those who see in every hour and in every moment of the existence of the Church, from its beginning until now, the overruling, almighty hand of him who sent his Only Begotten Son to the world to become a sacrifice for the sin of the world, that as he was lifted up so he, by reason of his righteousness and power and the sacrifice which he has made, might lift up unto God all the children of men who would hearken to his voice, receive his message, and obey his law.[1]

As usual, I share such quotes, for when I have searched them out they are something from my files "for your files." Special quotes are better shared than stored.

Confessing God's hand likewise includes acknowledging, accepting, and avowing that God comprehends all things (see 2 Nephi 2:24; 9:20; D&C 38:2; 88:6; 130:7; Moses 1:6). It would be difficult to worship Him, wouldn't it, if things were otherwise? If He were preoccupied with overwhelming problems of His own, or if God were distracted or not really "on top of things," how could we worship Him unreservedly and trustingly?

Granted, it is puzzling for us as to just how God's foreknowledge leaves uncompromised our moral agency, yet we continue daily to choose for ourselves, reassured that on the great judgment day, with a fulness of facts, "all men" shall confess that He "is God" and that His judgment is "just" (Mosiah 27:31). What a moment that will be!

Agency, accountability, and opportunity will be shown to have been sufficiently mixed with mercy, so that God's justice will be openly attested to by all. No dissent is mentioned. Of one thing we can be confident; our acknowledgment should consist in much more than resignedly or humorously saying: "Of course I believe in free will. What choice have I?" [2]

Included in that vast and later concourse in which *every* knee shall bow and *every* tongue confess that Jesus is the Christ will be a previously un-meek group. These will be those who have lived without God in the world and who have been unacknowledging of anything spiritual. Yet they too will concur that God is God; likewise, that His justice and mercy are perfect, and that His works are just (see Alma 12:15).

One real risk we run daily is that we will be miffed with God over this or that. Brigham Young counseled us that when one is "a little distrustful with regard to the providences of God, in entertaining a misgiving in his heart and feeling with regard to the hand of the Lord towards him . . . his mind will begin to be darkened. . . . If there is a misgiving in the heart with regard to confidence in our God, do you not see that there is a chance for one to slide a hair's breadth from the truth? This gives power to the enemy, and if we are de-coyed in the least from the path of duty, do you not perceive that it produces darkness?" [3] This is part of taking up the cross daily (see Luke 9:23). In discipleship, it is the "cross before the crown."

Meanwhile, acknowledging God's deliberate hand like-wise avows that God has His own timetable. In fact, "all things must come to pass in their time" (D&C 64:32).

God has even anticipated our failures and has made ade-quate allowances for them. The Prophet Joseph Smith said: "The great Jehovah contemplated the whole of the events con-nected with the earth, pertaining to the plan of salvation, be-fore it rolled into existence, or ever 'the morning stars sang to-gether' for joy; the past, the present, and the future were and are, with Him, one eternal now. . . . He knew . . . the depth of iniquity that would be connected with the human family, . . . and has made ample provision for their redemption." [4]

Imagine, "ample provision" even in the face of massive human error! So it is that God can realistically reassure us, "I am able to do mine own work" (2 Nephi 27:20, 21). His higher ways and purposes will triumph over the consequences of man's lower ways (see Isaiah 55:8–9). It is, in fact, the constant spreading of the consequences of man's lower ways that produces those circumstances which discourage us at times, causing some wonderment over the meaning and purposes of life.

Confessing or acknowledging God's hand also involves allowing for how deeply God is committed to our "moral agency" (D&C 101:78). It was in this connection that President Joseph F. Smith forthrightly disclosed his feelings about the verse we are discussing:

> The Lord is greatly displeased only with those who do not confess or acknowledge "his hand in all things, and obey not his commandments." Many things occur in the world in which it seems very difficult for most of us to find a solid reason for the acknowledgment of the hand of the Lord. [The only thing] I have been able to discover by which we should acknowledge the hand of God in some occurrences is the fact that the thing which has occurred has been permitted of the Lord.[5]

God's commitment to our moral agency is so much higher than, given our lower ways, we can even imagine! Some things clearly are permitted of God which are not approved of God:

> This was none of the good Lord's pleasure,
> For the Spirit He breathed in man is free;
> But what comes after is measure for measure
> And not God that afflicteth thee.[6]

Even so, confessing God's hand in all things surely does not mean, for instance, that His hand caused the great and terrible holocaust in which six million Jews perished. Instead, Enoch saw the God of Heaven weep over needless human suffering. Asked by Enoch why He wept, God declared that He had "[given] unto man his agency," also a "commandment that they should love one another . . . but behold, they are without affection . . . and the fire of mine indignation is kindled against them" (Moses 7:32–34).

Throughout history the Stalins, Hitlers, and Herods have made their awful choices and performed their cruel works for an awful season. Clearly, while God is over all things, He does not do our choosing for us. Rather, the rule is, "Nevertheless, thou mayest choose for thyself" (Moses 3:17). Nor does He shield us from all the consequences of our bad choices. So much of our knowing the bitter and the sweet consists of personally witnessing, if not experiencing, the consequences of both bad and good choices. Brigham Young counseled concerning our capacity to comprehend:

> It is like words in the wind to talk about the sweetness of the honeycomb to those who have not tasted the opposite. You may talk about the glory and comfort of the light to those who never knew darkness, and what do they know about it? Nothing. You might as well preach to those lamps. If we can realize that everything in all the eternities that ever were and ever will be is ordained of God for the benefit and glory of intelligent beings, we can understand why he said to Joseph, "Against none is my anger kindled, only those who do not acknowledge my hand in all things." Do I acknowledge his hand? Yes. I told you in your afflictions, drivings, persecutions, and all that has been grievous to be borne, that the hand of God was in that as much as it was in bringing forth his revelations and the Priesthood through Joseph. . . . So with "Mormonism:" every time they give it a kick, it rises in the scale of power and influence in the world.[7]

Clearly our appreciative acknowledgment of God's hand is justifiably called for. First, we are indebted to God not only for our very mortal existence but also even before that for our individual spirit births. Additionally, the Light of Christ "lighteth every man that cometh into the world" (see D&C

84:46; 93:2; John 1:9). This further, supernal blessing is also
provided by God's loving hand.

There are innumerable reasons to worship Him and to acknowledge His sustaining and expediting hand in all things,
including the provision of this habitable planet. "For the
earth is full, and there is enough and to spare; yea, I prepared
all things, and have given unto the children of men to be
agents unto themselves" (D&C 104:17).

And again, "I, the Lord, stretched out the heavens, and
built the earth, my very handiwork; and all things therein are
mine" (D&C 104:14).

Of the heavenly bodies He declared: "And any man who
hath seen any or the least of these hath seen God moving in
his majesty and power" (D&C 88:47).

"The fulness of the earth is [ours]" (D&C 59:16). Furthermore, it truly pleases God to have given "all these things
unto men" (D&C 59:20).

Confessing God's hand thus calls for an array of appreciation in response to all that our loving Father has given, does
give, and will yet give mankind. There is a tendency to acknowledge only "big blessings" without acknowledging the
multiplicity of "small blessings." Isaiah would doubtless include these latter in his acknowledging of the "multitude of
[God's] loving kindnesses" (Isaiah 63:7; see also D&C
133:52).

Really, even when we are reasonably dutiful, compared to
such a flow of divine generosities and benefactions "of what
have we to boast?" (Mosiah 2:23–24). King Benjamin so
stressed: "I say unto you, my brethren, that if you should ren-
der all the thanks and praise which your whole soul has
power to possess, to that God who has created you, and has
kept and preserved you, . . . if ye should serve him with all
your whole souls yet ye would be unprofitable servants"
(Mosiah 2:20–21).

By the way, several LDS scholars suggest that the words
of Benjamin's prayer may contain fragments of an ancient
Jewish prayer—unknown, of course, to Joseph Smith. In the
Jewish prayer of praise, the She-hecheyanu uses phrases like:

> *Praised* art thou,
> Lord our *God, King* of the
> Universe, who has *kept* us
> And has *preserved* us.
> And enabled us to reach
> *This* festival season.

King Benjamin, of course, speaks of:

> "thanks and *praise*" and of
> "that *God* your heavenly King
> who has created you and has
> *kept* and *preserved you* . . .
> and is *preserving you from day to day*
> . . . even supporting you
> *from one moment to another.*"

The parallels are interesting![8]

Therefore, whether in His granting us our daily bread, in lending us our momentary breath, or in providing our breath-taking views of the heavens, it is all one glorious gift from our Father! There is divine design in the vast galaxies as well as in the tiny DNA molecule.

Even so, God is not seeking praise from us for His sake. The praise is to be given for *our* sakes. It is for the good of our own souls that we need to so acknowledge His hand. Ingratitude can become so ingrown, otherwise.

Acknowledging gratefully all the grand realities brings more meekness. Proper acknowledgment "here and now" likewise prepares us to see His face "there and then" with pleasure, rather than shrinking from His piercing glance (see Enos 1:27; Mosiah 27:31).

It is a happy thought that once we regain our presently inaccessible memories of the first estate we will be fully informed. We will then be able to acknowledge many more now-forgotten blessings which were given us there.

As we reflect upon our profound blessings, even "through a glass darkly," how wonderful it is that God's "longsuffering" permits us, if we will, to develop a greater capacity to appreciate all He has done for us. Most of us are not only slow learners but even slower acknowledgers.

The process of working out our salvation requires both the loving-kindness and the longsuffering of the Lord. We can count on these divine attributes, though we do not regularly and openly acknowledge them. It is much the same as our not including in our evening and morning prayers expressions of gratitude for how the Lord has kept this planet, for one more day, just the right distance from the sun, so that we are neither frozen nor fried. We don't praise Him for these things, do we? But well we might!

Given the sheer volume of our blessings, perhaps we can be forgiven for not acknowledging all of them all of the time, but the failure to "count our blessings" at all is unforgivable.

More unfortunately, however, we seldom praise God for His longsuffering and loving-kindness upon which we profoundly and constantly depend. We get busy with the things and cares of the world, including the legitimate ones.

Take the case of Amulek, an essentially good man of substantial political and economic sway. At the time of his spiritual turning, however, he acknowledged, "I knew . . . yet I would not know . . . I was called many times and I would not hear" (Alma 10:6). Later Amulek was to lose his old friends, but he was to become a new and full friend of God. He was to lose His worldly wealth, but he would gain the riches of eternity. (See Alma 15:16.) Through Amulek, the Lord, in "loving-kindness," poured some of the most powerful teachings we find in all of scripture.

Imbedded in all of this need to confess God's hand is the reality of divine design in life's structure. President John Taylor spoke instructively about the practicality and spirituality of the plan of salvation:

> I know . . . we have our trials, afflictions, sorrows, and privations; we meet with difficulties; we have to contend with the world, with the powers of darkness, with the corruptions of men, and a variety of evils; yet at the same time through these things we have to be made perfect. It

is necessary that we should have a knowledge of ourselves, of our true position and standing before God, and comprehend our strength, our weakness, our ignorance and intelligence, our wisdom and our folly, that we may know how to appreciate true principles, and comprehend, and put a proper value upon, all things as they present themselves before our minds. It is necessary that we should know our own weaknesses and the weaknesses of our fellowmen; our own strength, as well as the strength of others; and comprehend our true position before God, angels, and men; that we may be inclined to treat all with due respect, and not to over-value our own wisdom or strength, nor depreciate it, or that of others, but put our trust in the living God, and follow after Him.

It is necessary, then, that we pass through the school of suffering, trial, affliction, and privation, to know ourselves, to know others, and to know our God.[9]

John Taylor asked a searching question: "Can we acknowledge the hand of God? Can I acknowledge his dealings with my family? . . . While you reflect on this, and find that you have many hard things to cope with, can you say, 'It is the hand of God; let him do as seemeth him good?' "[10]

Given such transcendental and individual purposes for this life, no wonder we pass through such a variety of vexing expectations. Coming to "put our trust in the living God" is not the work of a day or a season. Instead, this mortal school continues to the very end, when the final school bell rings for each of us.

So let us gladly and frequently acknowledge God's hand in all things.

Given all the foregoing, when we "confess [or acknowledge] God's hand in all things" (D&C 59:21), we need to bear in mind the following:

- He permits some things to happen which may truly puzzle us.
- He will not force compliance, for He honors our moral agency: "Nevertheless thou mayest choose for thyself" (Moses 3:17).

- His purposes will finally prevail, and at the great Judgment Day all will acknowledge Him as God and acknowledge His justice and His mercy (Alma 12:15; Mosiah 16:1).
- As mortals we sometimes "blame" God for the miseries flowing from our many and interactive human mistakes. We will not always understand "all things" at the time, but we can still know that God loves His children (see 1 Nephi 11:17).
- God's omniscience permits Him to take all things into account. He is perfectly aware, perfectly loving, perfectly empathic. But He is also deeply committed to our moral agency and to our spiritual development. His interventions are His decisions, and they will always reflect His divine attributes at the center of which is His loving-kindness.

Though God may be filled with righteous indignation at mortal error over a particular circumstance, and He even weeps over human suffering, His plan of happiness will finally prevail. If there is to be any vengeance, it will be His. True, He may not take away our bitter cup, but He can help us to partake without becoming bitter. If we endure deprivation well, we will receive "all that my Father hath" (D&C 84:38). There isn't any more than that! In the midst of our difficulties He has told us "my grace is sufficient" for the meek (Ether 12:27).

I admire your inquiring mind, but even more I love you for your sweetness and steadfastness.

Grandfather

P.S.

So often you have voyaged in the world of books. The following quotation from another Emily (Dickinson), therefore, seems so appropriate to share:

> There is no Frigate like a Book
> To take us Lands away
> Nor any Coursers like a Page
> Of prancing Poetry—
> This Traverse may the poorest take
> Without oppress of Toll—
> How frugal is the Chariot
> That bears the Human soul.[11]

Notes

1. Joseph F. Smith, *Gospel Doctrine* (Salt Lake City: Deseret Book Company, 1986), p. 52.
2. Joseph Epstein, "Our Debt to I. B. Singer," *Commentary*, November 1991, p. 36.
3. *JD* 3:222.
4. *Teachings*, p. 220.
5. *Improvement Era*, vol. 20, July 1917, p. 821.
6. Rudyard Kipling, as quoted by Martin Sieff in "Prophetic Poet of Power and Peace," *Insight*, 5 May 1986, p. 79.
7. *JD* 6:148.
8. See FARMS, Working Paper, WEL, 8 sc.
9. *JD* 1:148.
10. *JD* 6:112.
11. Quoted in the *Atlantic Monthly*, January 1991, p. 62.

Cleaning Up for a Mission

Dear Robbie:

Apparently your friend is trying to get his life in order so he can go on a mission. Encourage him to stay close to his parents and bishop.

There is direction from President Brigham Young about prospective missionaries: "If the Elders cannot go with clean hands and pure hearts, they had better stay here and wash a little longer."[1] Though stern sounding, this is actually redemptively sweet counsel!

It is good you care about your friend and want him to have the special experience which awaits. Hopefully his "little longer" will pass quickly.

God bless you both.
Grandfather

Notes

1. *JD* 6:273.

The Highest Type of Intelligence

Dear Heather:

We read about the importance of having an "opposition in all things." Meaningful agency requires the existence of alternatives, among which we are to choose. Otherwise, "all things must needs be a compound in one." (2 Nephi 2:11.) This interesting phrase notes that but for the opposition there would be no holiness, no wickedness, no misery, no happiness, no good, no bad, no sweet, no bitter, no sense, and no insensibility. However, since things are not in such a compound, life is lively, especially given the reality of the multiplicity of choices and experiences facing us daily.

No wonder it is the adversary's pattern to try to blur the differences between the holy and the profane by creating situations of seeming ambiguity. It takes intelligence and faith in order to make one's way through it all.

The word *intelligence* as we encounter it in section 130, by the way, is not the usual "IQ" kind of measurement. This "intelligence" discerns, learns, and applies true and correct principles; it reflects a composite of knowledge and wise behavior. It combines cognition and application. This reflects the highest type of intelligence, and the blended result will rise with us in the resurrection (see D&C 130:18).

An individual who gains "more knowledge and intelligence" in this life will do it not only intellectually but also through his "diligence and obedience." The person who is thus progressing "will have so much the advantage in the world to come." (D&C 130:19.)

Eternal love,
Grandfather

P.S.

You spoke of the sarcasm of your friend. The cynicism of others can pain and disappoint us. However, I find it helpful to recall what someone once said: "Cynicism is nothing more than idealism gone sour."

What are your duties to your friend? Of such difficult moments, Brigham Young said: "Some do not understand duties which do not coincide with their natural feelings and affections. Do you comprehend that statement? . . . There are duties which are above affection."[1]

Notes

1. *JD* 7:65.

By the Spirit

Dear Ryan:

I'm glad your mission president emphasizes teaching by the Spirit!

We live and teach amid a wide variety of individual personalities, experiences, cultures, languages, interests, and needs. Only the Spirit can compensate fully for such differences. "The sword of the Spirit" is the penetrating "word of God" (Ephesians 6:17). Thus holy scripture and the words of living prophets occupy a privileged position and they also perform a special task. Teaching by the Spirit employs what the Prophet Joseph Smith called "the language of inspiration."[1]

However, being in an increasingly secularized world, we should not be unduly discouraged when "the natural man receiveth not the things of the Spirit of God: for they are foolishness unto him: neither can he know them, because they are spiritually discerned" (1 Corinthians 2:14). Many individuals simply refuse to be informed by the Spirit.

When speaker and hearer, or writer and reader, are spiritually conjoined, a special revelatory reciprocity occurs: "Therefore, why is it that ye cannot understand and know, that he that receiveth the word by the Spirit of truth receiveth it as it is preached by the Spirit of truth? Wherefore, he that preacheth and he that receiveth, understand one another, and both are edified and rejoice together." (D&C 50:21–22.) John Taylor elaborated: "There is no man living, and there never was a man living, who was capable of teaching the things of God only as he was taught, instructed and directed by the spirit of revelation proceeding from the Almighty. And then there are no people competent to receive true intelligence and to form a correct judgment in relation to the sacred principles of eternal life, unless they are under the influence of the same spirit, and hence speakers and hearers are all in the hands of the Almighty."[2]

The Spirit not only informs but it also *convinces!* The Spirit, for example, can convince the serious inquirer sufficiently to have him "experiment upon" the gospel. Then the prized, personal verification will come. The person comes to know for himself that these things are true (see Alma 5:46).

Brigham Young said, autobiographically, of the Spirit's convincing power:

> Anything besides that influence will fail to convince any person of the truth of the Gospel of salvation. . . . But when I saw a man without eloquence, or talents for public speaking, who could only say, "I know, by the power of the Holy Ghost, that the Book of Mormon is true, that Joseph Smith is a Prophet of the Lord," the Holy Ghost proceeding from that individual illuminated my understanding, and light, glory, and immortality were before me. I was encircled by them, filled with them, and I knew for myself that the testimony of the man was true. . . . My own judgment, natural endowments, and education bowed to this simple, but mighty testimony. There sits the man who baptized me, (brother Eleazer Miller). It filled my system with light, and my soul with joy. The world, with all its wisdom and power, and with all the glory and gilded show of its kings or potentates, sinks into perfect insignificance, compared with the simple, unadorned testimony of the servant of God.[3]

Whether transmitting or receiving, under the influence of the Spirit we hasten the precious process in which an individual is "quickened in the inner man" (Moses 6:65; see also Ephesians 3:16; Psalm 119:40). This involves high, spiritual drama. Yet when we speak about teaching by the Spirit it is not about a mystical process which removes responsibility from the missionary or teacher for prayerful and pondering preparation. Teaching by the Spirit is not the lazy equivalent of going on "automatic pilot." We still need a carefully worked out "flight plan."

Studying out something in one's own mind is, in itself, an invitation to the Spirit in our preparations as well as in our presentations. We must not err, like Oliver Cowdery, by taking no thought except to ask God for His Spirit (D&C 9:7). The Lord is especially willing to take the lead of an already informed mind in which things have been "studied out." Additionally, if we already care about those to be taught, the Lord can inspire us with any customized counsel or emphasis which may be needed.

In any case, we cannot be clinically detached when teaching by the Spirit. An example from the political world may help to make a point about the interactiveness of human feelings. When Winston Churchill was only twenty-three he wrote an essay on rhetoric which was never published but was found among his papers after his death. Therein he spoke of the role of feelings in communicating with others: "Before he can inspire them with any emotion he must be swayed by it himself . . . Before he can move their tears his own must flow. To convince them he must himself believe. . . . He who enjoys [this gift] wields a power more durable than that of a great king. He is an independent force in the world. Abandoned by his party, betrayed by his friends, stripped of his offices, whoever can command this power is still formidable."[4]

President Harold B. Lee gave us the clearer, spiritual equivalent: "You cannot light a fire in another soul unless it is burning in your own soul. You teachers, the testimony that you bear, the spirit with which you teach and with which you lead, is one of the most important assets that you can have, as you help to strengthen those who need so much, wherein you have so much to give."[5]

Proper feelings are most instructive when accompanied by the eloquence of personal example as one teaches with the added "authority of example." Then others can more easily "believe on [our] words" (D&C 46:14).

President Joseph F. Smith urged parents: "Teach to your children these things, in spirit and power, sustained and strengthened by personal practice. Let them see that you are earnest and practice what you preach."[6] Absent such visible, authenticating earnestness, so many presentations are thereby deprived of their desired influence even when content is commendable.

The early faith of the beginner often involves a special trust in the words of one already faithful: "Faith in the words alone of my servant" (Mosiah 26:15). "And if now thou sayest there is a God, behold I will believe" (Alma 22:7). Such discipleship brings its own rewards as such individuals are "blessed . . . because of their exceeding faith in the words alone which thou hast spoken unto them" (Mosiah 26:16). Some of your contacts and investigators will have a special regard for your words. They will trust and surrender.

By the way, the Spirit does not impose itself or linger with the unwilling. Resisted, it will quickly withdraw.

One of the primary functions of the Spirit is to bring things to our remembrance. A wise man said that we usually need to be reminded more than we need to be instructed.

The Spirit stimulates that pondering and remembering that encourages intellectual honesty. It was so with Amulek, who later candidly acknowledged that before his spiritual quickening he knew, and yet he would not know; he was called, and yet he would not hear (see Alma 10:6).

Little wonder that when we partake of the sacramental bread we ask to have the Spirit *always* with us. Only then are we safe; otherwise, without the Spirit, we are left to ourselves. Who would ever want to solo, anyway?

The Spirit brings instructive substance as well as instructive feelings: "These words are not of men nor of man, but of me: wherefore, you shall testify they are of me and not of man" (D&C 18:34). "Believe in these words, for they are the words of Christ, and he hath given them unto me" (2 Nephi 33:10). "The word had a . . . more powerful effect upon the minds of the people than . . .anything else" (Alma 31:5). "When a man works by faith he works by . . . words" (*Lectures on Faith* 7:3). "But this generation shall have my word through you" (D&C 5:10).

The following "Do's" and "Don't's" affect the climate. The "Do's" invite the Spirit, while the "Don't's" discourage it.

Do	*Don't*
1. Focus on the teaching moment by being settled and serene.	1. Be upset by Martha-like anxieties. Joseph Smith was once briefly ineffective after he and Emma had a disagreement. Inviting the Spirit is difficult, if we are crowded with other concerns.
2. Be meek, and "I will tell you in your mind" (D&C 8:2).	2. Try to impress in order to be heard or seen of men.
3. Have some eye contact with and listen to those being taught.	3. Be so busy presenting that either listening to the Spirit or to the students is not possible. Don't expect the class to listen to you when you are not listening to the Spirit.
4. Use inspired one-liners which will be remembered and retained.	4. Multiply words or concepts. Would we cherish the Sermon on the Mount if it filled three volumes?
5. Focus the substance of what is being presented.	5. Present a "smorgasbord," hoping someone will find something of value. If unfocused, this leaves the receivers uncertain.
6. Proffer relevant applications and implications of what is being taught.	6. Answer irrelevant questions no one is asking.

Do	*Don't*
7. Ask inspired questions.	7. Be afraid of questions or of saying "I don't know."
8. Be prepared to learn from what you say while under the influence of the Spirit.	8. Be afraid to ponder in front of the students.
9. Provide moments of deliberate pause during which the Spirit can supply its own "evidence of things not seen" (Hebrews 11:1).	9. Be afraid of inspired silences.
10. Let the doctrines speak for themselves. Brigham Young said: "Every principle God has revealed carries its own convictions of its truth to the human mind."[7]	10. End up "selling" the doctrines because of overanxiety; let the Spirit do the convincing. Professor Arthur Henry King wrote articulately of Joseph Smith's account of the First Vision: "When I was first brought to read Joseph Smith's story, I was deeply impressed. I wasn't inclined to be impressed. As a stylistician, I have spent my life being disinclined to be impressed. So when I read his story, I thought to myself, this is an extraordinary thing. This is an astonishingly matter-of-fact and cool account. This man is not trying to

Do	*Don't*
	persuade me of anything. He doesn't feel the need to. He is stating what happened to him, and he is stating it, not enthusiastically, but in quite a matter-of-fact way. He is not trying to make me cry or feel ecstatic. That struck me, and that began to build my testimony, for I could see that this man was telling the truth."[8]
11. Bear your testimony appropriately and specifically.	11. Just say "I have a testimony."

Since we can only speak the smallest part of what we feel, anyway, we should see to it that the "smallest part" is taught by the Spirit.

Thanks for your patient perusal of this long letter, which now ends in the words of Jacob: "O be wise; what can I say more?" (Jacob 6:12.)

Blessings on you, your companion, and those you teach.

I love you.
Grandfather

P.S.

Like the rest of us, you will feel inadequate and inarticulate at times, but with the Spirit, though, "a poor speaker may suppose his language is nothing, that it is very small, yet God can make it pierce like a javelin to the hearts of Saints and sinners."[9]

Notes

1. *Teachings*, p. 56.
2. *JD* 17:369.
3. *JD* 1:90–91.
4. William Manchester, *The Last Lion: Winston Spencer Churchill Alone, 1932–1940* (Boston: Little, Brown and Co., 1988), p. 210.
5. "Stand Ye in Holy Places," *Ensign*, July 1973, p. 123.
6. "Worship in the Home," *Improvement Era*, December 1903, p. 138.
7. *JD* 9:149.
8. *The Abundance of the Heart* (Salt Lake City: Bookcraft, 1986), pp. 200–1.
9. Heber C. Kimball, *JD* 10:45.

Selfishness—the Persistent Feature

Dear Lauren:

The hardest part of taking up the cross "daily" is to overcome one's reflexive, persistent selfishness. Allowing for its many faces, selfishness is the most profound, pronounced, and persistent feature of the natural man. George MacDonald observed that it is as if, each morning, we need to break all over again the crust of self that has gathered afresh about us.[1] The steady secretions of selfishness will continue to re-encrust us until we put off the natural man and woman—firmly and finally!

Admired by all the rest of us are the men and women who are low demanders but high performers. These unselfish few are so quietly contributive. Without excessive expectations, these individuals often go unheralded, yet they make up part of the critical mass of human goodness. For them, a word of spiritual direction is sufficient—like the Roman centurion who asked only a healing word from Jesus, not His presence (see Matthew 8:5–13).

As neighbors, these individuals make high but quiet contributions. They also make low demands of others and even of the Church. They are meekly content with "what is allotted" to them (Alma 29:3–4, 6). They take their trials in stride, pressing forward on the straight and narrow path. They are unsurprised by adversity and manage to live in "cheerful insecurity."

In contrast, the natural man never picks up the cross. His is the "sorrowing of the damned," which involves regret but not necessarily over the sin itself. Instead, it is because these sorrowers can no longer take pleasure in sin (see Mormon 2:13). Quite a difference, for the natural man still clings, not to the cross, but to his old ways!

Those forces which appeal to our selfishness and sensuality

often conspire against us. There is a striking sameness in the combines of craftiness formed by designing men in any age (see D&C 89:4). Their craftiness is often subtle and always focuses on things which appeal to the natural man. Anyone who challenges that rigid pattern of things or who goes against the grain of that intellectual fashion is highly resented as an alien intruder!

But Paul is right, the fashions of this world will pass away (see 1 Corinthians 7:31). Some men save neckties, awaiting the time when they will be in fashion again. However, when the life-style and fashions of this world disappear, it will be irrevocable.

Daring to be different from the fashions of this world is to become fashionable for that realm in which true beauty and spiritual symmetry are ever honored.

I love you and the joy in life you have always displayed in your sweet appreciativeness!

Love,
Grandfather

Notes

1. See C. S. Lewis, ed., *George MacDonald Anthology* (New York: Macmillan, 1947), p. 138. (Hereafter cited as *MacDonald Anthology*.)

Truth from the Earth

Dear Michael:

I'm so pleased with your studies in the Book of Mormon! How blessed we are to have it available to read again and again! However, it wouldn't have done as much good, would it, for the Lord to have restored the Book of Mormon before the invention of printing presses? Truth not only had to come "out of the earth"; it also had to spread across the earth "like a flood"! (Isaiah 29:4; 2 Nephi 3:20; Moses 7:62.)

By the way, Hyrum Smith is one of Church history's significant but modest men. How he loved and supported Joseph! He watched the coming forth of the Book of Mormon and stood by it. On March 16, 1839, he wrote from Liberty Jail to Clarrinda, a girl being cared for by the Smiths, and to a daughter, Lovina. Though he was victimized by weeks of suffering, notice what Hyrum (in a letter to a Sister Grinnals, 16 March 1839) recommended with the few words the space allowed him:

[To Clarrinda:] "Let mother give you one of the Books of Mormon and write your name in it. I want you to seek every opportunity to read it through. Remember me both night and morning in your prayers."

[To Lovina:] "You may have my small Book of Mormon. You must try to read it through. Pray for your father that the Lord may help him to come home."

Special thanks for being so loving and thoughtful to your younger sister over the years.

Much love,
Grandfather

P.S.

As you study the Book of Mormon you will find that
gospel doctrines are like diamonds with many facets. Some
are hidden from our initial view. An experience can cause the
glint of the gospel to illuminate a dimension of a doctrine
previously unappreciated. The doctrines, therefore, are to be
pondered, turned over and around, in order to see their full
beauty and new and added relevancy.

Faith in God's Timing

Dear Brian:

Faith in God includes faith in His timing. Frankly, some of us have some difficulty with this significant dimension of faith. We clearly prefer our own time to His "own due time."

Wilford Woodruff recalled that he heard his pioneer brethren discussing the yet-to-be-built Salt Lake Temple, sometimes speaking of using softer building materials. He listened patiently, but

> When in the western country, many years ago, before we came to the Rocky Mountains, I had a dream. I dreamed of being in these mountains, and of seeing a large fine looking temple erected in one of these valleys which was built of cut granite stone, I saw that temple dedicated, and I attended the dedicatory services, and I saw a good many men that are living today in the midst of this people. . . . And whenever President Young held a council of the brethren of the Twelve and talked of building the temple of adobe or brick, which was done, I would say to myself, "No, you will never do it," because I had seen it in my dream built of some other material. I mention these things to show you that things are manifested to the Latter-day Saints sometimes which we do not know anything about, only as they are given by the Spirit of God.[1]

He didn't challenge his sincere peers. He just bided his time—and granite it was! Brigham said: "When the Temple is built I want it to stand through the millennium, in connection with many others that will yet be built, . . . We have decided that this Temple shall be built of this beautiful granite rock, which, I think, will please everyone."[2]

There were those who had private feelings concerning the

new calling of Assistant to the Twelve announced in 1941. They sustained the Brethren when that new calling was initiated, but they were wondering inwardly why instead more Seventies were not called; they were to be called upon instead of "any others" (D&C 107:38). For thirty-five years the calling of Assistant to the Twelve served the Church well, including acting as a seedbed for numerous Apostles and even for members of the First Presidency. Then, in 1976, under inspiration President Spencer W. Kimball began to reconstitute the Seventies into what has since become the much-needed, plural Quorums of the Seventy.

Similarly, Brigham Young reported having strong feelings in a conversation involving Elder McLellin's failure to understand the full significance of the apostolic calling in relationship to being a high priest. This was indicated by McLellin in a group discussion which included the Prophet Joseph. Brigham did not dispute McLellin but, instead, he held his tongue briefly. Waiting soon paid off, for then the Prophet Joseph spoke. Brigham reported: "Said Joseph, 'Will you insult the priesthood? Is that all the knowledge you have of the office of an Apostle? Do you not know that the man who receives the Apostleship, receives all the keys that ever were, or that can be, conferred upon mortal man?' "[3]

Similarly John Taylor and other early missionaries bided their time, as the Prophet directed, before having authorization to preach the gathering. But though the early brethren followed the Prophet Joseph's instructions, members themselves received spiritual intimations of the gathering. Concerning this, John Taylor said: "Joseph Smith might tell us it was not wisdom to preach the principle of gathering; but we could not help the Lord revealing that principle through the medium of the Holy Ghost, which was to teach us all things."[4]

Commenting further, President Taylor observed: "That was all well enough, but we could not keep it from the people. Why? They had received the Holy Ghost, and that took of the things of God and showed them to the people, and you could not hide the gathering from them."[5] In reciting the same account again, he noted that the previous situation was "just the same as I have to say today, that there are many things that I know of which I can only tell you when the time comes."[6]

Of course, there are those few who claim that the Holy Ghost leads them yet they do not follow the Brethren, an inconsistency which will grow among us.

Patience stretches our capacity to bide our time while both wondering and sustaining. This vital elasticity will be especially needed as part of maintaining faith in God's timing in the last days, during which "all things must come to pass in their time" (D&C 64:32).

How much this superb scripture portends for us as individuals and as a Church! It is one thing to agree with the general proposition that God's timetable is to prevail, and it is quite another to agree when the waiting or hastening rule is applied directly to us, isn't it?

I love you.
Grandfather

P.S.

While mentioning time, let me add that you will likely find the following to be true in your professional career: In your early years, you will gladly trade precious time for needed money; later, you will gladly trade money for needed, precious time!

Notes

1. *JD* 21:299–300.
2. *JD* 11:372.
3. *JD* 1:137.
4. *JD* 24:199–200.
5. *JD* 15:171.
6. *JD* 25:180.

Witnesses

Dear Kimball:

Your question about being personal witnesses is so short and specific! I'll try to be likewise.

Even those Nephites "who have seen me and know that I am" were nevertheless told: "And again, *more blessed* are they who shall believe in your words because that ye shall testify that ye have seen me, and that ye know that I am. Yea, blessed are they who shall believe in your words." (3 Nephi 12:1–2, emphasis added; see also D&C 46:13, 14.)

On another hemisphere Thomas received similar instruction: "Jesus saith unto him, Thomas, because thou hast seen me, thou hast believed: Blessed are they that have not seen, and yet have believed" (John 20:29).

Of course, as prized as the personal reliable witnesses of others are to us, progression in personal, spiritual knowledge is still highly desirable. As the Samaritans who now had heard Jesus personally said to one who earlier had borne witness, "Now we believe, not because of thy saying: for we have heard him ourselves, and know that this is indeed the Christ, the Saviour of the world" (John 4:42).

We know when we know! We also know how we know. Yet we find it difficult to explain spiritual things to others. Certain things are "spiritually discerned" (see 1 Corinthians 2:14). The undiscerning do not understand—they are much like the man who "cut open the ball in search of its bounce."

I love you and appreciate your inquiring mind.

Grandfather

The Recognition That Counts

Dear Elizabeth:

Enduring well is so much more than simply waiting out the passage of time—just as good citizenship is much more than simply paying taxes.

Some of us endure life's major afflictions better than we endure small slights. How do we feel, for example, when we are unfairly unmentioned in a public litany of appreciation? Though we may appear outwardly unoffended, do we brood inwardly? Was the oversight deliberate or merely forgetful? For the meek, however, any regret is minimal and concern is reserved for the one who did the overlooking, lest he be embarrassed.

For those too concerned with credit, the mortal books, however well kept and well intended, are incomplete anyway. They could not stand a real "outside audit." The real and complete Book of Life is kept elsewhere! One day it will be opened and we will all be judged out of it (see Revelation 20:12). There will be no challenge then to the justice or mercy of God (see Mosiah 27:31; Alma 12:15).

I have become more and more persuaded that our transparent drives for recognition are somehow subtly bound up with our seeming need to verify that we matter. We wish neither to be taken for granted nor to be regarded as a mere cipher. Attention becomes a form of validation.

Yet Jesus was regarded "as a thing of naught"! (1 Nephi 19:9; see also Mosiah 3:9.) He was considered by most to be a mere man (see Mosiah 3:9). However, He knew who He was and what He had to do. We can know, too. Mortal mathematics, however, is forever mistaking who and what counts. Even so, we should be more quick to express genuine appreciation to others. The arithmetic of appreciation is far less practiced and known than the multiplication tables.

I love you and your constant concern for what is right.

Grandfather

P.S.

Sometimes our excessive assertion of verbal comments may be a search for self-validation or verification. Some thus "stake out space" as a means of saying, "I am." "I matter." "Notice me." Other times, of course, our assertions are simply a matter of routine participation, representing a genuine desire to make a contribution. Unfortunately, a few times, by our assertions we are seeking to control or exercise dominion, a far different thing from simply wishing to make a contribution.

Occasionally our assertions represent the feverish search of our "memory bins" for items which seem to "match up" with the topics at issue. Doing this in order to impress others with our retrieval capacity or to prove that we can still hold our own may be understandable but not commendable.

Ridding Ourselves of Fear

Dear Erik:

We are told that "perfect love casteth out fear" (1 John 4:18; Moroni 8:16). For all of us who still have some fears, how can this really occur?

If our love of God is sufficiently deep, then we will be sufficiently assured of His enveloping loving-kindness. With this perspective, our fears can shrink. Dread can dissolve. Additionally, there need be no *ultimate* fear for mankind's future solely because of *proximate* circumstances, vexing and besetting as the latter may be.

Amid our "small moment," we can know that what we are passing through can be "for [our] good" (D&C 122:4, 7). We thus love God sufficiently to trust in His perfect love for us even when we do not know the full meaning of the difficult moment.

Granted, because we now look "through a glass, darkly" (1 Corinthians 13:12), we do not see the details very clearly. Nevertheless we can surely distinguish between light and darkness, between the revelations and despair. We can understand that some of our tribulations come because "all these things shall give thee experience" (D&C 122:7).

When our love of God is not sufficiently developed, He may choose to wrench our heartstrings. Amid the anguish we can at least acknowledge that it is His hand doing the wrenching! President John Taylor quoted the Prophet Joseph Smith thus: "You will have all kinds of trials to pass through. And it is quite as necessary for you to be tried as it was for Abraham and other men of God, and (said he) God will feel after you, and He will take hold of you and wrench your very heart strings, and if you cannot stand it you will not be fit for an inheritance in the Celestial Kingdom of God."[1]

Since God is perfect in His goodness, "let him do what seemeth him good" (1 Samuel 3:18).

Full submissiveness, whatever life's local "weather," would still leave us "calm as the summer's morning." By way of example, deeper love of God and others will aid us, when we are roiling with resentment, to meekly say our equivalent of, "Father, forgive them; for they know not what they do" (Luke 23:34).

How different, really, are those who mock God because of the human predicament from those who mocked Jesus on the cross, even as He was thereby assuring them of their personal immortality?

We are to "look to God and live" (Alma 37:47). Peter advised that we are also to cast our cares upon God, because He cares for us (see 1 Peter 5:7). Why not do the same with our fears?

Yet, hesitantly, we poise on the brink of real submission. But since God has given us life and all else we have, anyway, how can we really withhold ourselves, our attitudes, or our substance from His shaping love? Our degree of submissiveness thus becomes a true reflection of the degree of the consecration and love we have developed for Him. Similarly, the dimensions of our fears expose the degree to which our love for Him remains yet to be developed.

I love you.
Grandfather

<hr />

Notes

1. *JD* 24:197.

A Portrait of Jesus

Dear Katie:

From all the insights and disclosures found in the Lord's various revelations, entreaties, and commentaries there emerges a clear, beckoning, and powerful portrait of Him; it forms a marvelous montage!

He is a Lord of "loving-kindness" (Isaiah 63:7; D&C 133:52); "I . . . delight to honor those who serve me" (D&C 76:5); "The fulness of the earth is yours" (D&C 59:16); "There is enough and to spare" (D&C 104:17); "Any . . . who have seen any or the least of these hath seen God moving in his majesty and power" (D&C 88:47); "It pleaseth God that he hath given all these things unto man" (D&C 59:20); "I have stretched forth mine hand almost all the day long" (Jacob 5:47; see also 2 Nephi 28:32); "Eye hath not seen, nor ear heard . . . the things which God hath prepared for them that love him" (1 Corinthians 2:9). The repentant and fully faithful shall receive "all that [the] Father hath" (D&C 84:38). Finally, the faithful will be "clasped" in the waiting and "open arms" of Jesus! (Mormon 5:11; 6:17.)

Remember, with his perfected empathy Jesus has a special feeling and understanding, acquired "according to the flesh," for those who feel forsaken and alone. Do we all need to experience, in some degree, feeling forsaken or alone? Apparently, for there are some things Jesus would have His most devoted disciples know firsthand. Secondhand won't do.

Given the history of His generosity and beckoning to us, no wonder the Lord could say with full, cumulative justification, "O Jerusalem, Jerusalem, . . . how often would I have gathered thy children together even as a hen gathereth her chickens under her wings, and ye would not!" (Matthew 23:37.)

By the way, whenever I try substituting my own name for *Jerusalem*, long-suffering Jesus' question becomes even more searching and moving.

Much love,
Grandfather

Some Won't Let God Be God

Dear Ryan:

A word about those who, in their own minds, will not let God be God. They would have Him possessed of only fragmentary, inferential foreknowledge by being unable to see the future, thus qualifying His omniscience. No wonder King Benjamin pleaded with us to believe "that man doth not comprehend all the things which the Lord can comprehend" (Mosiah 4:9).

God is also regarded by some as being unable to do His work. This view so diminishes God that He soon becomes a vague concept, a periodically comforting nightlight instead of a bright, universal light! With vagueness comes impersonalness. The fact that He is the literal Father of our spirits becomes neglected.

Hence the rejection of God's own descriptions of His capacity and personality can ultimately lead people to a rejection of Him—and, as well, to the denial of Jesus' atonement by their "denying the Lord that bought them" (2 Peter 2:1). Surely this includes the unfortunate questioning by some of the literalness of Jesus' suffering for our individual sins.

When individuals deny the attributes of Deity they are in effect denying the essential capacity of Deity. Ironically this causes some to lack real faith in God. Others, of course, deliberately keep their belief in God rather vague—to protect what little attachment to Him they still have. Still others apparently believe in a God who is "over the hill," having been able to deliver ancient Israel out of Egypt but being no longer able to deliver us from evil or death.

Actually, we only know about God what He chooses to reveal to us. Hence we'd best pay very careful attention to what He *has* revealed!

Helpful as it is for so many purposes, logic by itself is an inadequate tool in our seeking to know God and His personality. Abstractions and extrapolations will not suffice—only revelation will do! Furthermore, it is essential, along with knowing that God "is," to know what He is like and also what His purposes are. He describes these to us, for we cannot discern them unaided.

God is involved, for instance, with a plurality of worlds and in overseeing an ongoing plan of salvation (see D&C 76:24; Moses 1:33, 38). It is vital for us to know about this in order to understand the nature of the human experience and the nature of the universe. God is perfect in His love, justice, empathy, kindness, goodness, longsuffering, and patience. This too is vital information, for as we know this we can have full confidence not only that *He is*, but also in what *He is like*. It is likewise concerning His capacity to accomplish His work (see 2 Nephi 27:20–21).

How can we truly say that we accept Him as a God of truth if we deny what He says about himself?

Some people resent the Latter-day Saints because what we believe is so stunning and mind-expanding. Certainly our individual hypocrisies and shortcomings are made more glaring by all the bold and demanding doctrines in which we believe. Our theological certitude is also sometimes seen as smugness. It certainly helps if absolute truth is possessed by those who are, in turn, especially loving and behaving.

It is a sad fact that these latter feelings constitute real stumbling blocks to some.

Why was Jesus, himself, a stumbling block? (See 1 Corinthians 1:23.) First, He violated the narrow expectations people had about the Messiah. Understandably, the local establishment wanted relief from an oppressive military government. Jesus spoke, instead, of relief from everlasting death, the last and greatest oppressor. The local populace were not willing to follow His instructions, by means of which they could have personally verified who He was (see John 7:17). They were always "looking beyond the mark" (Jacob 4:14). Christ fulfilled prophecy after prophecy, but this went unnoticed. Jesus was also a stumbling block because He challenged hypocrisy (see Matthew 23:15, 27).

Thus, while to the Jews Jesus was a "stumbling block," to the Greeks He was "foolishness" (1 Corinthians 1:23). A short while later, Greek philosophy's impact on Christianity was to be immense and insidious.[1]

Though we walk by faith, not by sight (see 2 Corinthians 5:7), faith still produces its own form of reliable evidence. Such evidence, which is "spiritually discerned" (1 Corinthians 2:14), will of course be rejected by some (see Helaman 8:24).

Korihor was not unlike some of the world's philosophers. Korihor's pattern of argument apparently attracted quite a following. He spoke vehemently in saying that "no man can know of anything which is to come" (Alma 30:13). In fact, "ye cannot know of things which ye do not see" (Alma 30:15). These and other arguments shook those who were not spiritually established. They still do today.

Perhaps Korihor's most telling argument was one which led to much immorality by "telling them that when a man was dead, that was the end thereof." (Alma 30:18.) Some commendably avoid immorality though they live without any hope of immortality. But for others, the removal of a belief in personal accountability and immortality brings a life-style of selective iniquity (see Alma 30:18). Iniquity, in turn, brings despair (see Moroni 10:22).

Stumbling blocks not only cause us to lose our balance; they can also cause us to give up. Stumbling blocks can be overcome only when they are recognized for what they are. For instance, our narrow thinking can be enlarged, as was Moses', by learning things we "never had supposed" (Moses 1:10).

By contrast, despairing man is turned inward on himself and is focused on the here and the now. He is thus encouraged to please himself and to go for the moment, because "there can be no Christ" (Alma 30:12–13) and therefore no rescue from the human predicament. Perhaps some in their minds refuse to let God be God because they do not wish to be His accountable children.

Eternal love,
Grandfather

Notes

1. See Stephen E. Robinson, "Warring Against the Saints of God," *Ensign*, January 1988, p. 39.

We Can Choose Joy

Dear Martha:

Your observations concern a most profound question. How can we ever expect to have a fulness of joy unless *all* those we love share that joy? In other words, how can there be "fulness" if there is "incompleteness"? How can loving parents, for instance, have a fulness of joy if their prodigals never really come home? Your cousin once asked a similar question.

As in all things, what God has revealed to us is our truest guide, though more is yet to come. We know for a certainty that God weeps over the unnecessary suffering of humanity. Enoch saw Him weep! (See Moses 7:28.) Can the Lord ever have a fulness of joy in view of such sadness?

The resurrected Jesus did: "And they arose from the earth, and he said unto them: Blessed are ye because of your faith. And now behold, my joy is full." (3 Nephi 17:20.)

After all that we can do to help another, that person receives what he or she has openly and persistently chosen, which reflects the actual and undoubted desires of his heart (Alma 41:5–6). All are "free to choose" for themselves (2 Nephi 2:27; Moses 3:17). Choices have consequences. In that sense, how we use our own moral agency is our personal determination. It cannot be otherwise, for "God will force no man to heaven." Neither, however, will He allow "Hell to veto Heaven."[1]

Besides, as Allen Bergin wrote, even an omnipotent and omniscient God cannot choose to create another God, except with the full cooperation of that individual.[2] Burdened Moses genuinely wished "that all the Lord's people were prophets" (Numbers 11:29). Yet Moses could not wish into general existence such devotion and qualifications.

We weep, and should, for those who suffer because of sore sin. Moreover, we should practice longsuffering and personal patience to maximize every opportunity for their in-gathering. However, some will still refuse to "come in from the cold." Finally, each of us receives the dominant desires of his heart. Furthermore, a very generous God will finally provide a degree of glory for all but a very few. As mercy overpowers justice, each and all of us will rejoice in the degree of divine mercy bestowed upon us. (See Alma 34:15.)

Thanks for your cheering ways over the years.

Love,
Grandfather

P.S.

By the way, C. S. Lewis also noted that some would try to use our earthly empathy and sympathy to blackmail us. Yet "the day must come when joy prevails and all the makers of misery are no longer able to affect it . . . I know it has a grand sound to say ye'll accept no salvation which leaves even one creature in the dark outside. But watch that sophistry or ye'll make a Dog in a Manger, the tyrant of the universe."[3]

My own guess is that our present regrets for spiritual shortfalls will eventually be refined into a celestial empathy which recognizes moral agency's irrevocable relationship to eternal joy. Brigham Young once described, for example, how God's pure affection still manages to make room for righteous indignation: "The principle of pure affection is the gift of God, and it is for us to learn to control it and to exercise proper dominion over it; and if we are faithful, we shall see the time when we can say, as our Father in Heaven says, I am angry with the wicked; I hate their works, and mine anger is kindled against them. Is there any malice or wrath there? No; for it is written that the Lord is angry, but sins not."[4]

Notes

1. C. S. Lewis, *The Great Divorce* (New York: Macmillan, 1965), p. 120.
2. Letter to the author, 11 September 1991.
3. *The Great Divorce*, p. 121.
4. *JD* 6:149.

Wrong Way, Wrong Expectation

Dear Brittany:

Yes, most of the human family, if they think about it at all, expect God to give man the maximum moral agency but without human misery and divine interference!

This expectation is particularly evident in our time, when "every man walketh in his own way" and after the image of his own god (D&C 1:16). There are historical parallels: "In those days there was no king in Israel, but every man did that which was right in his own eyes" (Judges 17:6).

We prefer our own ways, for "all the ways of a man are clean in his own eyes; but the Lord weigheth the spirits" (Proverbs 16:2).

Instead, what is wanted is that spiritual condition in which "every man might speak in the name of God the Lord, even the Savior of the world" (D&C 1:20).

Without spiritual submissiveness, however, this can't happen. It can come about only if we follow our Great Exemplar, whose submissiveness made Him our Saviour: "Yea, even so he shall be led, crucified, and slain, the flesh becoming subject even unto death, the will of the Son being swallowed up in the will of the Father" (Mosiah 15:7).

I love and admire you.
Grandfather

P.S.

So far as influencing others lastingly is concerned, it is always so much better to touch hearts than to twist arms.

Spiritual Experiences

Dear Robbie:

You asked whether God gives signs only to those who do not need them. I would put it otherwise. God gives signs only to those who will not misuse or misread them.

Brigham Young cautioned about the need for confidentiality in such sacred matters, noting that, if we prove trustworthy, "there is an eternity of them to bestow upon you." But we should learn "to have integrity . . . and know when to speak and what to speak, what to reveal."[1]

On another occasion he waxed introspective on this very topic:

> And I will say, as I have before said, if guilt before my God and my brethren rests upon me in the least it is in this one thing—that I have revealed too much concerning God and his kingdom, and the designs of our Father in heaven. If my skirts are stained in the least with wrong, it is because I have been too free in telling what God is, how he lives, the nature of his providences and designs in creating the world, in bringing forth the human family on the earth, his designs concerning them, &c.[2]

Having apparently heard someone who seemed to delight in telling of his, you also asked about spiritual experiences.

President Marion G. Romney observed that we would have more spiritual experiences if we did not talk about them so much!

As if having them were more important than benefitting from them, some lust after spiritual experiences rather than desiring the substance of such experiences: "Ask not, that ye may consume it on your lusts, . . . but that ye will serve the true and living God" (Mormon 9:28). Perhaps, in recounting their spiritual experiences, some may unconsciously wish to demonstrate their ascendancy; just as some academics, in a sort of intellectual imperialism, enjoy the knowing more than they enjoy utilizing what is known. This illustrates the old problem of the desire for preeminence, which can take many forms.

Brigham Young urged us to keep spiritual confidences, saying: "Just as fast as you will prove before your God that you are worthy to receive the mysteries, if you please to call them so, of the kingdom of heaven—that you are full of confidence in God—that you will never betray a thing that God tells you—that you will never reveal to your neighbor that which ought not be revealed, as quick as you prepare to be entrusted with the things of God, there is an eternity of them to bestow upon you."[3]

President John Taylor observed that prophets often know more than they are free to say. He noted that Joseph Smith said that "he felt himself shut up in a nutshell . . . it was difficult for him to reveal and communicate the things of God, because there was no place to receive them. What he had to communicate was so much more comprehensive, enlightened, and dignified than that which the people generally knew and comprehended, it was difficult for him to speak; he felt fettered and bound, so to speak, in every move he made, and so it is to the present time."[4]

Our readiness to receive is gauged by God, but sometimes we are pushy. President Young wisely counseled: "We are like children who want the looking-glass to play with, and who cry for the sharp razor and for the moon they see reflected in the water, desiring them for play-things. Let us take such a course that God will have confidence in us, and then we shall receive all we need, all we desire and ask for."[5]

Eternal love,
Grandfather

Notes

1. *JD* 4:371–72.
2. *JD* 8:58.
3. *JD* 4:371–72.
4. *JD* 10:147–48.
5. *JD* 4:79.

Goodness Comes in Many Degrees

Dear Sarah Jane:

There are as many degrees of doing good as there are ways of doing good. Some things are of only momentary value, while others are of eternal significance. Some activities bring "joy for a season" only—their satisfactions are fleeting (3 Nephi 27:11). Eating the miraculous loaves and fishes was a supernatural event, yet the participants' natural hunger was only temporarily satisfied. Worse still, soon many of those very beneficiaries rejected the Bread of Life, who could have helped them to never again hunger spiritually. Yet they "walked no more with him" (John 6:66).

The legitimate work of this world really does matter, being quite necessary for this mortal season. Some people give themselves to it with great devotion and intensity. They are, "in their generation" (in their framework of time and perspective), more intensely devoted to their fleeting causes than the "children of light" (Luke 16:8) are sometimes to their grander cause. We should do much better, given our wider and deeper perspective, as a result of seeing "things as they really are" (Jacob 4:13). Without the gospel's precious perspective, however, as one wit observed, we might end up enthusiastically building toothpick factories in times of famine!

Though the good work of the world does not compare to the work of eternity, it often lessens needless human suffering and may preserve, even increase, human freedom. It is reassuring to know, as King Benjamin said—and he knew both significant political and significant spiritual power—"When [we] are in the service of [our] fellow beings [we] are only in the service of [our] God" (Mosiah 2:16).

Furthermore, God "delights" to honor *all* those who serve Him in various degrees and ways (see D&C 76:5). How could it be otherwise? He is the loving and merciful Father of us all and takes joy in all the good works of all His children.

How quickly and generously an outpouring and generous God blesses all those who obey Him! In one such episode, "even the high priests and teachers were themselves astonished beyond measure" (Helaman 3:25). We're not quite prepared for all God will do for us when we are ready to receive. True, blessings come by obedience to God's laws, but the gear ratio between our obedience and His blessings is generous indeed!

I love you for doing your part over the years and for coping with occasional disappointment.

Grandfather

Freedom Requires Self-Discipline

Dear Ashley:

Yes, just as you said in your delightful buoyancy, we do live in an incredible time. In recent years we have witnessed the deepening and broadening of some human rights in a few lands, especially for those who have lived unfree through the long, dark Cold War. This truly is a special cause for rejoicing!

However, since you ask, I do not think that in the human experience such exhilarating seasons go unchallenged for long. It's ironical that oppressive old ways can still triumph over new freedoms, producing unwanted and unintended outcomes. Into the new circumstances can come the old miseries. If, for instance, the old "gulag" societies merely give way to new Sodom-like societies, the human misery index will still be unacceptably high. If expanded freedom, anywhere, merely heralds drugs, immorality, and pornography, the net gain is questionable. Unions and alliances held together by dictatorial powers may break up into cultural, tribal factions as nations within nations war against each other. Forgive my senior citizen perspective!

If what now follows seems a little preachy, it is not directed at you. Please scan it to see if it contains any useful rejoinders, for you must speak to your own generation.

Maintaining true freedom requires much self-discipline. Permissiveness cannot sustain true liberty for long. While we may poke justifiable fun at how cumbersome, unfree economic systems could take over the Sahara Desert and within three months produce a shortage of sand, likewise, marketplace economies with no standard or heart or "safety nets" can generate their own sad consequences.

In Sodom they probably had absolute free speech, but nothing worth saying! On the other hand, an otherwise permissive society, which tolerates almost everything, usually will not tolerate speech that challenges its iniquity. Evil is always intolerantly preoccupied with its own perpetuation.

We are fortunate that there is substantial free speech in our own American nation. Yet many Americans are less and less able to express themselves through traditional forms of rational speech. Instead, some turn to gross ways of acting out their feelings—poor substitutes for genuine speech. Shocking crudity is far from being redeeming fluency!

The instructions to Adam and Eve about the garden earth, by the way, have not been rescinded. They were, and we are, to dress it—not destroy it. They were to take good care of it instead of abusing it. Our increasing interdependence on this planet makes some forms of individual selfishness the equivalent of a runaway personal bulldozer. If we have no concern for the generations to follow, the means are at hand to tear up the terrain much more than was ever possible anciently. Today's polluter or terrorist, for instance, can claim the lives of so many more than a mad owner of a longbow could have done centuries ago!

Can people consistently believe there can be rampant pornography without increases in child and spouse abuse? Likewise, if we celebrate selfishness, should we then wonder why the "love of many waxes cold"? (See Matthew 24:12; Joseph Smith—Matthew 1:10.) How much of the self-discipline necessary to sustain civilization can survive surging selfishness? Whence will come the emancipation proclamation for those held by the slavery of obscenity? Never expect obscenity and pornography to contain any signs of genuine empathy, a quality in short supply anyway.

Grossness in conduct is usually preceded or accompanied by grossness in language. Instead of employing beauty and variety, obscenity exhibits poverty of expression. What jars is not only the mounting crudeness but also the increasing sameness—like the indistinguishable grunts of a herd in a hurry to worship afresh at the shrine of sensualism.

When we lionize bizarre behavior, temper tantrums, and selfishness in various superstars, should we be surprised at the spreading of similar conduct? Should we applaud or should we pity someone for shooting himself in the foot?

We spend billions for the rightful rehabilitation of victims of plagues, but only comparative pennies to preach prevention. Jeers even greet those who advocate healthy abstention from various self-destructive acts.

Those determined to escape the present by using alcohol and drugs will ruin the future too. Those who have made themselves "past feeling" will not have the empathy to prepare an acceptable future for others (see 1 Nephi 17:45; Ephesians 4:19; Moroni 9:20).

In any case, we cannot expect to live in a time when "men's hearts shall fail them" (D&C 45:26) without expecting the faithful to have a few fibrillations of their own!

May you continue to be a light. Be grateful for life without demanding too much of it; rich, then, will be your rewards.

Much love,
Grandfather Neal

Giving and Receiving Feedback

Dear Andrea:

You commented on the challenge of giving and receiving feedback, which can come to us from many sources. Unfortunately, simply because of its source we may discount feedback which contains a needed insight. When it comes from loved ones (as in the case of Moses' father-in-law), this usually makes it easier to receive.

In view of your interest in discussing corrective counsel, a special illustration from the political realm follows. Clementine Churchill, loyal and able, loved her remarkable husband, Winston, enough to remonstrate with him occasionally. During the dark days, when his special leadership counted for so much, she wrote Winston a loving letter of reproof:

> My Darling,
>
> I hope you will forgive me if I tell you something I feel you ought to know.
>
> One of the men in your entourage (a devoted friend) has been to me and told me that there is a danger of your being generally disliked by your colleagues and subordinates because of your rough, sarcastic and overbearing manner. . . . I was astonished and upset because in all these years I have been accustomed to all those who have worked with and under you, loving you—I said this, and I was told "No doubt it's the strain."
>
> My Darling Winston. I must confess that I have noticed a deterioration in your manner; and you are not as kind as you used to be.
>
> It is for you to give the orders and if they are bungled—except for the King, the Archbishop of Canterbury and the Speaker, you can sack anyone and everyone. Therefore with this terrific power you must combine

urbanity, kindness, and if possible Olympic calm. . . . I cannot bear that those who serve the Country and yourself should not love you as well as admire and respect you—

Besides, you won't get the best results by irascibility and rudeness. They will breed either dislike or a slave mentality. . . .

Please forgive your loving devoted and watchful
                                    Clemmie[1]

Delightful and insightful, isn't it?

                              Your loving and admiring
                              Grandfather

Notes

1. Mary Soames, *The Biography of a Marriage: Clementine Churchill* (New York: Paragon House, 1988), p. 383.

For the Perfecting of the Imperfect

Dear Lauren:

May I convey a few words about life in the Church. The Church in its totality is, of course, a composite of several essential things. It involves true and transcending *doctrines* which answer man's most searching questions. It involves the *ordinances* necessary to salvation and exaltation as well as to our happiness here. It involves *divine authority*, resting on the foundation of Apostles and prophets and the priesthood *keys* they hold to administer in all those ordinances and to teach and preach all those doctrines. It is also a *community of saints*, a way of nurturing each other, of doing good and of organizing our love.

The Church is established for *"the perfecting of the Saints"* (see Ephesians 4:11–12). But it is filled with imperfect people, something for which regular allowance should be made.

The Church and its people also have a destiny: "And it came to pass that I, Nephi, beheld the power of the Lamb of God, that it descended upon the saints of the church of the Lamb, and upon the covenant people of the Lord, who were scattered upon all the face of the earth; and they were armed with righteousness and with the power of God in great glory" (1 Nephi 14:14).

It is not a static thing. Indeed, prophecies indicate that the Church will grow numerically but also that its faithful people will become sanctified spiritually, after having been tried in all things (see D&C 105:31–32; 136:31).

Members write their own spiritual records by receiving the ordinances and doctrines; through Christian service; through worship, including temple worship; by studying the scriptures; and by carrying out their duties. Thus we are all located at various and disparate stages in the process of becoming the men and women of Christ (3 Nephi 27:27).

In this community of Saints there are many opportunities to nurture, to serve, to help each other; but also to be helped. The Church provides a system of leadership and authority by means of which the usual *vertical nurturing* occurs. But we all have firm, additional, and clear obligations to each other in what has been called *horizontal nurturing.* Moreover, these relationships are not casual. Some duties are even received by covenant.

We often provide each other with the necessary clinical material to help us grow and develop, providing opportunities to serve, to forgive, and to learn from each other. Therefore it is very important that we make allowance for the fact that while the Church is "for the perfecting of the saints," it is not composed of perfected people who have already arrived spiritually. This reality requires making allowance for each other's imperfections—even in the context of perfect doctrines.

Because the Church involves organized love, if we are meek and responsive we are moved, beyond the frequency of our random impulses, to serve and to do good by being part of a structured and reminding system of watch-care for each other and for nonmembers as well.

The Church is not a democracy, however. Why would one want to belong to a church anyway if he could make it over in his own image, instead of developing the image of Jesus Christ in his countenance? (See Alma 5:14.)

While the Church provides many satisfactions, there are more than occasional frustrations. There are no perfect parents or bishops; no perfect Relief Society, Young Women, Primary, or stake presidents. Or General Authorities! There are many, however, who are serious about moving forward quietly "on the way to perfection," and they show it in their lives!

I love you.
Grandfather

Suffering and Moral Agency

Dear Heather:

If God is good and if He loves His children, why does He permit so much suffering, especially among little children? This is a real concern, isn't it?

The first fundamental fact, on which so many other facts turn, is that God leaves us "free to choose." Many of us think we understand that doctrine, but we have not really examined its full implications. Clearly, moral agency is severely and constantly abused, and never more than when that abuse causes children to suffer so needlessly and cruelly! But the human suffering which we ourselves generate—and this is so much of the grim and grand total—is not an indication of God's indifference. Rather, it is the measure of man's inhumanity to man. God's empathy is not to be defined by man's lack of empathy or by our sometimes stupid and cruel use of moral agency!

All of us should be very careful, therefore, about seeming to lecture God on suffering. God actually weeps over the suffering of His children. Enoch saw it! (See Moses 7:28–29.) He questioned God about those divine tears—especially in view of God's omnipotence and His omniscience. Why cry over one people on one planet—especially in view of how far God's vast creations stretch out?

The Lord rehearsed for Enoch that humanity and this earthly habitat are "the workmanship of [God's] own hands," and, further, that He gave us our knowledge and our agency. Most strikingly, the Lord then focused on the fact that the human family should love one another and should choose God as their Father. The two great commandments! Then the Lord lamented, yet "they are without affection, and they hate their own blood" (Moses 7:32–33).

Granted, God has set limits on wickedness before. He

intervened in Sodom and Gomorrah and, even more dramatically, in Noah's time. Children born into Sodom and Gomorrah in Lot's day had no meaningful moral agency. President John Taylor observed: "Hence it was better to destroy a few individuals, than to entail misery on many. And hence the inhabitants of the old world and of the cities of Sodom and Gomorrah were destroyed, because it was better for them to die, and thus be deprived of their agency, which they abused, than entail so much misery on their posterity, and bring ruin upon millions of unborn persons."[1]

In Noah's time, the "violence" and "corruption" were likewise so bad that God intervened. Certainly Christ's coming again in power and majesty will constitute an unparalleled intervention!

Meanwhile, some say the scale of suffering in the world calls for divine intervention now. Comparatively, they reason, what is the loss of a little choice if it will save so much suffering?

So many do suffer innocently and awfully because of the mistakes of others, including children, whose suffering makes us all especially ache. Remember Jesus' own sharp utterance about those who cause children to suffer? Better that a millstone were hung about their necks and they were drowned! (See Matthew 18:6.)

Even so, as the Mortal Messiah, Jesus did not intervene to stop all human suffering, did He? It was not Jesus' lack of compassion for the afflicted but their own lack of faith which actually kept healing miracles from being performed in some situations (see Matthew 13:58). His interventions result from His determinations and differentiations; these are not always clear to us.

Besides, how would we really feel about our Father and His plan of salvation if we had no meaningful moral agency? Wouldn't some be even more angry with God—at least later on? Instead, we will all later acknowledge His mercy and justice (see Mosiah 16:1; 27:31; Alma 12:15).

Put boldly, when the Father rejected Lucifer's offer that "not *one* soul shall be lost" (Lucifer would surely have "made the trains run on time"), the grim possibility then existed that *all* could be lost! Everything was at risk! The possibility apparently existed that, even amid the Atonement, even Jesus might "shrink" (D&C 19:18).

Since God can override the adversary to ensure that we are not tempted above that which we can bear (1 Corinthians 10:13), why not override human suffering—at least at some peril point? You noted tenderly the starving children in the sub-Sahara. One of nature's most ironical indicators is the bloated belly of a starving child.

Clearly, the world is full of pain and real suffering, ranging in degrees from a mere cut finger to the protracted agony of those starving, innocent children. Therefore is it realistically possible to square the existence of meaningful agency with the avoidance of any suffering by the innocent?

But even if we had the power to act, where would we mortals agree to fix the peril point? Where would we draw the line, the crossing of which would cause God to intervene automatically? Only if suffering is life-threatening? And, if so, should intervention be as frequent for the ninety-year-old as for the nine-year-old? How about nine hundred for aging Methuselah?

Should God intervene to prevent the psychological scarring of a child because of parental bickering? And how would a divine decree against marital strife be enforced? In fact, should there be any human suffering at all, even that shared suffering which Paul described as "common to mankind"? (1 Corinthians 10:13.) Clearly, some suffering is customized to the development of discipleship for the mature. Should all others, however, receive no mortal experience to enlarge their empathy? What would immortality among resurrected beings be like without developed empathy?

What of those dying of the dreaded AIDS? Should God remove all possibilities of sexual immorality and drug use? Should future parents be forced to be concerned with the consequences for their children of their behavior today? A remedy for AIDS would certainly end some sore suffering, wouldn't it? Hopefully, one will be found, and soon, especially for the sake of the innocent.

Perhaps God should swiftly depose all political rulers who

neglect human rights? Or those who allow the deterioration of the soil, thereby making famine inevitable? Or those who spend on unneeded armaments taxes which might have gone to aid and relieve suffering? But how can God remove all dictators without himself being dictatorial?

Besides, since suffering is relative, will God then be equally obliged to answer, in the affirmative, all petitions for relief? If not, how can He be just? Some feel they suffer because they need a second car or did not get the desired date to the prom. If, in the end, we merely say "Leave it to God," are we not better to leave all to God to begin with?

To some, God's longsuffering makes Him seem too much like an uninvolved, constitutional monarch off somewhere in space. He is not detached, however. He has told us He has no plans which do not involve His children. He loves us, and everything He does is truly "for the benefit of the world" (2 Nephi 26:24).

In fact, He has some clear and announced purposes as to this mortal experience. "Let us prove them herewith"; "I will chasten my people"; "Behold, I will try their faith and their patience"; "All these things shall give thee experience and shall be for thy good"; "Nevertheless, thou mayest choose for thyself"; and so forth. These are all part of the sobering stuff of life.

However, faith in God includes faith in His purposes as well as in His timing. We cannot fully accept Him while rejecting His schedule. We cannot worship Him but insist on our plans.

Perhaps with this dispensation's greater global awareness—along with its lively and commendable interest in liberty and justice—there was a special receptivity for receiving and pondering that revelation which reassuringly declares that all children who die before the age of accountability are saved in the celestial kingdom (D&C 137:10). Talk about safety nets! Furthermore, all will finally and justly be judged "according to their works, according to the desire of their hearts" (D&C 137:9).

In any case, all will ultimately acknowledge that God is God and that He is perfect in His justice and in His mercy (see Mosiah 16:1; 27:31; Alma 12:15). For all to agree that God is just in all His works foretells a remarkable awareness and appreciativeness! The trouble is that for most of us awareness comes later!

When we are finally permitted to recall our first estate we will praise God even more for His arrangement of the second estate. Right now, as you pointed out, it can be tough going—with each of us having a share of pains and puzzlements. Meanwhile, however, so much suffering can still be avoided! If we repent, for instance, we do not need to know "sore" and "exquisite" suffering (D&C 19:15-17).

Furthermore, we should do more, as individuals, to reduce suffering by being "anxiously engaged" in good causes (D&C 58:27). We can work against famine, disease, child abuse, pornography, sexual immorality, or drugs—those fashionable fountainheads of so much needless human misery!

There is certainly no need to feel helpless. Instead, there is every reason to be helpful. We cannot affirmatively affect everything, but we can do some things.

So it is that, before we put all of our disappointment upon the Lord for what we perceive to be His failure to intervene, we ought first to look to ourselves. There are so many opportunities to do good and to relieve human misery directly. Yet, alas, most of us are under-involved.

Meanwhile, mankind remains "free to choose." Herod chose to slaughter a large number of innocent children. Herod's savagery, and so much that preceded it, were doubtless included in Jesus' touching and revealing lamentation, "O Jerusalem. . . ." (Matthew 23:37). When agency goes awry, agony awaits.

Of course, if we wish, we can "refuse to be comforted," as Enoch refused at first. Yet after he received wider, revealed perspectives, he rejoiced. (See Moses 7:44, 55-67.) May it be so for us all!

I love you for your empathy, so highly developed in one so young.

Grandfather

Notes

1. John Taylor, *The Government of God* (Liverpool: S. W. Richards, 1852), p. 53.

The Inexhaustible Gospel

Dear Brian:

You observed at our last grandparents' fireside that I remain excited about the gospel even though I have been "at it" for a long time. True! I agree with President George Q. Cannon, who observed:

> It is a characteristic of the Gospel of Jesus Christ to not be easily exhausted; on the contrary, it is always attractive. You hear it today, as you heard it thirty or thirty-five years ago, and it possesses as many charms and as many attractions now as then; repeating it does not wear it out—does not make the subject threadbare—does not deprive it of its interest; but, on the contrary, its interest increases as years roll over our heads; as they pass by, our interest in the work of God, and our love for it, and our appreciation of its greatness, increase.[1]

We may become exhausted in His service, but we will never exhaust His restored gospel! Frankly, we have not even inventoried the gospel harvest basket, which is such a "good measure, pressed down, and shaken together, and running over" (Luke 6:38).

Eternal love,
Grandfather

Notes

1. *JD* 11:169.

The Apostleship

Dear Grandchildren:

I am glad that you first knew me as a grandfather, since I shall always be your grandfather. This fact has already given me great joy and fills me with rich anticipation. Later, as you matured, it was humbling to see your appreciation and respect for the calling of the apostleship inexplicably given to me.

It has been quite a few years now since that call came. Yet I still feel unready and unable. You may wonder why this calling has made me, and I expect others of the Twelve, feel perpetually inadequate.

Consider these statements about the holy apostleship. The first is from the Prophet Joseph, as reported by Brigham Young:

> All the Priesthood, all the keys, all the gifts, all the endowments, and everything preparatory to entering into the presence of the Father and of the Son, are in, composed of, circumscribed by, or I might say incorporated within the circumference of, the Apostleship. . . .
>
> Said Joseph, ". . . Do you not know that the man who receives the Apostleship, receives all the keys that ever were, or that can be, conferred upon mortal man?"[1]

President Young also spoke his own view:

> Now, brethren, the calling of an Apostle is to build up the kingdom of God in all the world: it is the Apostle that holds the keys of his power, and nobody else. If an Apostle magnifies his calling, he is the word of the Lord to this people all the time, or else he does not magnify his calling—either one or the other.

If he magnifies his calling, his words are the words of
eternal life and salvation to those who hearken to them,
just as much so as any written revelations contained in
these three books (Bible, Book of Mormon, and Doctrine
and Covenants). There is nothing contained in these
three books that is any more revelation than the words of
an Apostle that is magnifying his calling.[2]

As they honor Him, the Lord honors the men so called,
especially in their collective capacity, as in this sweeping and
sobering prophecy: "And it came to pass that I saw and bear
record, that the great and spacious building was the pride of
the world; and it fell, and the fall thereof was exceedingly
great. And the angel of the Lord spake unto me again, saying:
Thus shall be the destruction of all nations, kindreds,
tongues, and people, that shall fight against the twelve apostles of the Lamb." (1 Nephi 11:36.)

Thus the office and calling of the holy apostleship is such
a sacred and special thing. No wonder its recipients feel in
awe of it! No wonder, too, that the only Presidents of the
Church are those seasoned by years of service as Apostles.
Elder Orson Hyde so observed: "It is generally the case . . .
that when an individual is ordained and appointed to lead the
people, he has passed through tribulations and trials, and has
proven himself before God, and before His people, that he is
worthy of the situation which he holds."

These few become, successively, the presiding high priests
of The Church of Jesus Christ of Latter-day Saints at that
moment when the other Apostles, who hold the keys latently,
place hands upon the senior's head to set him apart.

Referring to such a person, Elder Hyde further stated
that "one that understands the Spirit and counsel of the
Almighty, that knows the Church, and is known of her, is the
character that will lead the Church."[3]

The scriptures state that the man and woman of Christ
will be easily entreated (see Alma 7:23)—meaning approachable, open to petitions. But being "easily entreated" does not
necessarily mean we should be "easily persuaded." One can
be approachable without being naive. A person can be a good

listener without believing all that is communicated; he can hear a cause without being captured by the cause. But if one is unavailable or unheeding he cannot fairly judge either a cause or a pleading. Nor can he develop the needed understanding or empathy.

The Twelve, for example, were warned not to "serve tables" (Acts 6:2). Serving tables would actually be so much easier and clearly more visible than is carrying certain heavy responsibilities, as Moses finally did—he would hear "every great matter" and ponder all the "hard causes" (Exodus 18:22, 26). The Twelve must do as Moses did—delegate the small causes. This can be done without their being insensitive and unaware, while still being open to consideration. The Supreme Court doesn't have to hear every case in order to effect the flow of the law.

Beyond this, each Apostle can and should have circles of friendship and personal Christian service to help keep him attuned and sensitive. These can be part of his helpful sampling of conditions in the Church.

Much love,
Grandfather

Notes

1. *JD* 1:134–35, 137.
2. *JD* 6:282.
3. *JD* 1:123.

Continuing in Well-Doing

Dear Erik:

A question lovingly asked: Did your concerns, which you candidly shared, develop after you had done your own duty fully?

Expressing frustrations may let off steam all right, but often it is steam which might have been used instead to propel us forward. Sometimes, in expressing our gripes, you and I are merely leaving dirty laundry at someone else's feet for them to worry about—and without even turning the socks inside out!

When we really care, we will try to transform our complaints into recommendations and our observations into solutions. Thus striving to be helpful is part of discipleship's taking "thought" and continuing "as you commenced" (see D&C 9:5, 7).

Continuing is part of being "anxiously engaged" and of not growing weary of well-doing (see D&C 58:27; 64:33).

Much love,
Grandfather

P.S.

You may remember these lines recited by the buoyant Apostle, LeGrand Richards. They apply to all of us:

For every worry under the sun
There is remedy, or there is none.
If there be one, hurry and find it.
If there be none, never mind it.[1]

Notes

1. *Church News*, 31 March 1979, p. 4.

The Spirit World

Dear Timothy:

Is one reason we are not told more about the details of God's work in the spirit world perhaps the intimidating larger scale of things there? The scope of the work there is so large that it might embarrass those of us here. Probably twelve times the earth's present population live there. For sure, twelve times as many Presidents of the Church in this dispensation alone are in residence and at work there! Perhaps God thus protects us in our present provinciality from feeling diminished by considerations of scale.

Much of our continuing to work out our own salvation in the spirit world consists of our further correcting our personal deficiencies. If, for instance, we fully accept Christ as our Savior, this includes accepting the fact that He asks us to become more like Him (see 3 Nephi 27:27). Clearly, in this rigorous process, not all gets done on this side of the veil of death.

It also helps to be reminded of what characterizes some of those in the terrestrial kingdom: "These are they who are not valiant in the testimony of Jesus" (D&C 76:79). One dimension of not being "valiant" is a lack of a real, personal effort to emulate Jesus (see 3 Nephi 27:27). It is one thing to acknowledge Jesus as Lord and Savior, but another to worship Him to the point of striving to become more like Him. Only the valiant really do the latter.

Instead of the stereotypic, simplistic view we sometimes have of life in the spirit world—one never-ending Sunday School class—human interactions are at work there, just as here. Further choices are to be made, associations to be developed, and opportunities to be responded to.

We do not now know precisely how God handles things in the spirit world so that life there is an extension of walking by faith. Death does not suddenly bestow upon the disbeliever full awareness of all reality, thereby obviating the need for any faith. Instead, what follows death is a continuum of the basic structure in mortality—until the Judgment Day, when every knee shall bow and every tongue confess that Jesus is the Christ (see Romans 14:11; Philippians 2:10; D&C 76:110). Until then, we "walk by faith, not by sight" (2 Corinthians 5:7).

How will God ensure this condition in the spirit world? We do not know. Yet He has certainly so handled the second estate in relation to the first estate, hasn't He? The memories of the first estate are not accessible in the second estate. The spirit world will be so arranged that there will be no legitimate complaints later over the justice and mercy of God (see Mosiah 27:31; Alma 12:15).

Furthermore, the gospel, when preached in the spirit world, will bring the same responses as here: "some believed the things which were spoken, and some believed not" (Acts 28:24).

Eternal love,
Grandfather

"Why" Questions

Dear Emily:

When you and I ask "why" questions of the Lord it is helpful to remember that the prophets themselves have asked "why" questions. Enoch asked the Lord, in view of His omnipotence and omniscience, why He wept (see Moses 7:28–29, 31). Joseph Smith asked a "why" question in the form of "how long"—how long would the Lord stay His hand from protecting His people (see D&C 121:1–3).

Enoch asked the Lord why He had called him, in view of his personal deficiencies (Moses 6:31). Moses asked much the same question, noting his own lack of articulateness (see Exodus 3:11; 4:10). He also asked the Lord, having seen the earth and its inhabitants, why He had made the earth (see Moses 1:30).

Nephi, though very righteous, was apparently very concerned with his remaining minor imperfections. He asked why his heart wept, why his soul was filled with sorrow, and why he yielded to temptations. (See 2 Nephi 4:26–27.)

Gideon, at a time when ancient Israel was being oppressed, asked why the Lord seemingly was not with them in their trying circumstances (see Judges 6:13).

The "why" question from prophets thus usually reflect their concerns over their personal inadequacies, wonderment about afflictions, and puzzlement over the Lord's timing. Or they seek clarifying information from the Lord concerning His purposes and His plans.

The most significant and poignant "why" question ever posed, of course, was that posed by Jesus on the cross as He felt forsaken near the end of the Atonement. "And about the ninth hour Jesus cried with a loud voice, saying, Eli, Eli, lama sabachthani? that is to say, My God, my God, why hast thou forsaken me?" (Matthew 27:46.)

No one was more entitled to ask why. Yet He submitted.

Therefore, given our "why" questions and those which even prophets ask, how vital it is that we personally do all we can to understand God's overall plans and purposes! How important, too, that we make allowance for His timing and likewise for His capacity to work purposefully with us and through us—even in the midst of our inadequacies and incomplete understanding!

Your loving Grandfather

Trials Are for Noticing

Dear Elizabeth:

Please don't blame yourself for noticing life's trials. We're expected to. We should have faith and even some understanding amid trial, but realistically we cannot expect to be clinically detached. We can't be observers and involved soldiers at the same time. Otherwise, the test would not be a full test—with all the tingling. Can it be "a fiery trial" (1 Peter 4:12) if one scarcely feels the heat?

This is not to say that a person need lose composure. If his pride is sorely wounded, how he handles the wound is the test. It is the sharp cuts which get our attention, mobilizing our resentments, feelings, and tendencies. When we are being thus wounded, taking our own scientific measurements at the same time is not objectively possible.

Of life's developmental opportunities there are surely "enough and to spare," even in our regular relationships with each other, to vex us.

Yes, as you lament, so many of the games adults play are but more sophisticated versions of a child's pride at play—"It's mine!" "No, it's mine!" "It's my turn!" "No, it's mine, you just had yours!" Hurt feelings; being left out; it's not fair; and so forth.

I am so glad you are becoming ever more conversant with the gospel's richness. You will become even more excited about the gospel in the years ahead. Momentum isn't just for sports!

Much love,
Grandfather

P.S.

William Law observed that "pride is only the disorder of a fallen world, it has no place among other beings; it can only subsist where ignorance and sensuality, lies and falsehood, lust and impurity reign."[1]

Notes

1. William Law, *A Devout and Holy Life* (Grand Rapids, Michigan: Sovereign Grace Publishers, 1971), p. 100.

No Cleanup in Sight

Dear Kimball:

So you waded through my little, and now old, book about Sodom! Hard reading—and not a pretty scene!

Yes, Sodom and Gomorrah had three sister cities, making a total of five "permissive" cities in these ancient plains. Today, permissiveness is pervasive. Would that there were only five cities so grossly affected!

We wonder, don't we, what would constitute today's critical mass of those sufficiently righteous? What would compare to the Lord's ten in order to forestall destruction?

Mosiah felt it was not common that the "voice of the people" was contrary to the will of God. But "if the time comes . . . , then is the time that the judgments of God will come" (Mosiah 29:26, 27).

The spreading oil slick of pornography, for example, carries with it terrible consequences such as bizarre and oppressive sexual behavior, child and spouse abuse, and ultimately a loss of the capacity to love. Unfortunately there is no "superfund" available to underwrite the cleanup of this destructive ooze. In fact, the funding flows in just the opposite direction, as that ancient cartel of lust and greed has significant sway once again. Meanwhile those coated in the awful ooze of pornography are effectively beached, and on filthy shores. Spiritually speaking, they can never take wing again until the ooze is finally cleaned off—"every whit"! It is a tender and commendable thing when volunteers clean off sea fowl after an oil spill. Where, however, is similar devotion displayed for those slimed over by pornography?

Irreligion has become very bold. It is more and more openly resentful of religion. In effect, irreligion has told religion to "go to the back of the bus" and to be quiet! In the inspired United States Constitution there is not, and could not really be, an "establishment clause" prohibiting the assertive ascendancy of irreligion or of strident secularism.

It would have been just like local, secular government, way back then, to criticize Noah for building an ark with timber which might have been utilized to expand the local zoo! On the other hand, had Noah lived in our highly regulated day, he probably would have been refused a building permit!

With confidence in your ability to make your way through it all.

Eternal love,
Grandfather

P.S.

Our perfect Father does not expect us to be perfect children yet. He had only one such Child. Meanwhile, therefore, sometimes with smudges on our cheeks, dirt on our hands, and shoes untied, stammeringly but smilingly we present God with a dandelion—as if it were an orchid or a rose! If for now the dandelion is the best we have to offer, He receives it, knowing what we may later place on the altar. It is good to remember how young we are spiritually.

Gaining Spiritual Knowledge

Dear Peter:

Let's go right to your major point concerning intellectual dissenters.

The gospel requires us to yield our minds as well as bend our knees. Minds are often more arthritic than knees. No wonder we are to seek to obtain the "mind of Christ" (1 Corinthians 2:16). Yielding intellectually, but only partially, is often the problem. There is the intellectual equivalent of Ananias and Sapphira's holding back a portion of their money (see Acts 5:1–11). Such holding back may be motivated by a mistaken notion that by so doing a person somehow preserves his individuality or demonstrates his God-given agency.

Individuals who thus hold back often demand to know more before they obey more. Their minds seek to run far ahead of their confirming behavior. They prefer exciting exploration to plodding implementation.

The real method of acquiring spiritual knowledge is clearly laid out for us by Alma (see Alma 32). It features what may at first seem to be an unexciting sequence: desiring to believe, giving place in order to experiment, believing, and knowing. There is no easy leap from deep doubt to deep knowledge. In between lies the terrain which requires the steady doing of God's will.

It is a merciful provision that, even if at first we have no more than a "desire to believe," or even if we begin with only a "particle of faith," we can still commence (Alma 32:27). But we must "give place" for the process. This means giving place in our hearts, minds, schedules, and life styles in order to make room to "try the experiment of its goodness" (Alma 34:4). Giving place and so experimenting is no small thing for some who really struggle with taking this simplest step.

Subsequently, by our nurturing the seed carefully and by experiencing for ourselves, belief grows into confirmed faith, and faith grows into knowledge. Personal verification thereby occurs "in that thing"—meaning, in the principle which is specifically being obeyed and applied. Other principles or doctrines await the same process of personal verification.

Instead, however, some people want to skip the seemingly plodding "spiritual method." As already pointed out, they are so busy surveying large, intellectual tracts that they fail to cultivate even a small behavioral tract. Theory rich and data poor! Intellectual speculation is easy, and compared to steady, spiritual submissiveness it makes few demands. The speculators end up "looking beyond the mark" (Jacob 4:14), staring beyond the obvious. Jesus confirmed that only if we will "do" will we then "know" (John 7:17).

Your namesake, Peter, affirmed that if we have obeyed and are thereby developing certain qualities of character we will not be unfruitful in the knowledge of Jesus Christ (see 2 Peter 1:8). Once again, obeying is linked to enlarged knowing! Obedience is thus a true friend of intelligence, a fact which comes as a surprise to some.

Jacob warned about those who sought for that which they could not understand (see Jacob 4:14). Their zest for exploring and speculating is not matched by their enthusiasm for obeying and doing. Consequently, such individuals do not really come to know for themselves (see Alma 5:45–47). Without that personal witness they are ambivalent and unable to defend gospel truths or doctrines. It is people's incapacity to defend the faith, wrote George MacDonald, which can turn them into persecutors.[1]

Others have once known, but because of a subsequent failure to nourish their faith they have grown "weary and faint in their minds" (see Hebrews 12:3).

God wants us *to believe*, but He also wants us *to be,* to become. As we nurture our faith and gradually develop the qualities of Christ, everything becomes mutually reinforcing. Obeying leads to more knowing. More knowing leads to more obeying and more improving. More improving leads to more knowing and obeying. Finally, it's on to submission and consecration!

Yet it all starts with a simple desire to believe and with a humble willingness to give place in order to experiment upon the word of Christ—by doing!

Is it possible that an initial unwillingness to give place is a telling, early indicator of one's underlying stubbornness? Stubbornness often masquerades as individuality, causing some to hold back throughout life.

When people are not really willing to submit, even to a small degree, they will end up skimming, wearily and disappointedly, over life's surface. Emerson spoke of our growing "weary of the surfaces."[2] Soon the heat of life's sun scorches what little belief exists! (See Alma 32:38.)

I love you.
Grandfather

P.S.

Some, though decent and good, prefer the ambience of living in the general vicinity of the Lord's neighborhood. They do not really desire to go all the way home or to be "clasped in the arms of Jesus" (Mormon 5:11). But anything we "embrace" instead will keep us from the ultimate embrace with Him!

Notes

1. See *MacDonald Anthology*, p. 121.
2. Quoted in Richard Hazelett and Dean Turner, *Benevolent Living* (Pasadena: Hope Publishing, 1990), preface.

The Built-in Challenges

Dear Katie:

In his superb statement on the role of personal experience as encountered in mortal life Elder John Taylor was not recommending a wanton, prodigal search for indiscriminate experience.[1] Rather, he spoke to the reality that life has sufficient built-in challenges and trials for each of us such as are "common to man" (1 Corinthians 10:13). If we keep the commandments, we will not only pass safely through those experiences but will learn from them as well. However, the passage certainly can't be made without even noticing the trials. We're expected to notice them.

"There is an opposition in all things" (2 Nephi 2:11). All facts are demonstrated by "their opposites," said Brigham Young. He further counseled, "We find ourselves surrounded in this mortality by an almost endless combination of opposites, through which we must pass to gain experience and information to fit us for an eternal progression."[2]

As we pass through these opposites we can thereby achieve an enhanced appreciation for good people and good principles. Likewise we can thus increase our empathy for others, which is part of Elder Taylor's "treating all with due respect." The challenge is for us to be meek enough to learn from our own mistakes and right choices as well as from observing the experiences of others.

Out of life's experiences, said Elder Taylor, we can better comprehend the Lord, ourselves, and others. We can thus mark well our strengths, while noting and working on our weaknesses. We need neither depreciate our strengths nor overvalue them; similarly with the strengths and weaknesses of others.

Elder Taylor thus sets forth a healthy and practical view of the mortal school. It is in this school that our talents and

God's truths are necessarily mixed with time so that all who are willing learn by their own experiences (see Alma 32:34).

In this view of learning we can better ponder Nephi's harsh experiences with Laman and Lemuel, the tutoring experience Alma had with Amulek, the reconciliation of Jacob and Esau, and Rebekah's interesting and significant role, as a righteous woman, along with her prophet husband, Isaac.

Of course, it happens all the time that people pass through life without learning. Some simply will not "try the experiment" of the gospel's goodness (Alma 34:4). Others despair: "Are all men's lives . . . broken, tumultuous, agonized and unromantic . . . Who knows? . . . I don't know. Why can't people have what they want? The things were all there to content everybody, yet everybody got the wrong thing. I don't know. It's beyond me. It's all darkness."[3]

With experience, we also come to see that not all decisions are between stark black and white choices. Some choices are made between the varying shades of gray. We thus experience real choices, not merely abstract ones, and they bring varied consequences. How else could we learn to "put the proper value upon things"?

Brigham Young counseled persistently on this basic point:

> I will give you my reasons for this; if Adam had not sinned, and if his posterity had continued upon the earth, they could not have known sin, or the bitter from the sweet, neither would they have known righteousness, for the plain and simple reason that every effect can only be fully manifested by its opposite. If the Saints could realize things as they are when they are called to pass through trials, and to suffer what they call sacrifices, they would acknowledge them to be the greatest blessings that could be bestowed upon them. But put them in possession of true principles and true enjoyments, without the opposite, and they could not know enjoyment, they could not realize happiness.[4]

Only through these developmental experiences can we be made "perfect," or become, in terms of our individualized capacity, fully developed. As Elder George Cannon put it, "until every quality of our nature, of that God-like nature which we have inherited from our Father and God, shall be fully developed; until we shall be made capable of associating with God."[5]

The mortal school, properly attended to, thus produces special outcomes in its best pupils: "To be gentle and kind, modest and truthful, to be full of faith and integrity, doing no wrong is of God; goodness sheds a halo of loveliness around every person who possesses it, making their countenances beam with light, and their society desirable because of its excellency. They are loved of God, of holy angels, and of all the good on earth, while they are hated, envied, admired and feared by the wicked."[6]

This basic objective accords with what Brigham's beloved mentor, Joseph Smith, said: "If you wish to go where God is, you must be like God . . . [in] the principles which God possesses."[7]

What a sobering but encouraging view of life! No wonder we have a duty as neighbors to help each other get through this experience!

Thus self-knowledge, knowledge of our fellowman, and knowledge of God give us a more realistic sense of our true position, a comprehension of "things as they really are." (Jacob 4:13)[8] We thus truly desire, as John Taylor said, to "put our trust in the living God, and follow after Him."

Our gratitude to God will grow with our spiritual momentum and with our increasing comprehension of all that God and Jesus have done. This is why, in the world to come, we will praise Jesus "forever and ever," especially for His lovingkindness and longsuffering and for His atonement (see D&C 133:52; see also 1 Nephi 19:9). However, the "natural man" resists learning such spiritual things. Brigham Young explained:

Then instead of concluding that the Lord has drawn us into difficulties, and compelled us to do that which is unpleasant to our feelings, and to suffer sacrifice upon sacrifice to no purpose, we shall understand that He has de-

signed all this to prepare us to dwell in His presence. . . .
He has so ordained it, that by the natural mind we cannot
see and understand the things of God, therefore we must
then seek unto the Lord, and get His Spirit and the light
thereof, to understand His will. And when He is calling
us to pass through that which we call afflictions, trials,
temptations, and difficulties, did we possess the light of
the Spirit, we would consider this the greatest blessing
that could be bestowed upon us.[9]

Hence the learning experiences may sometimes be severe.
Orson Hyde taught: "Do you not see that the prodigal son
learned a good lesson in the school of adversity, which he
could not learn in his father's house. The spirit of rebellion
could not be made to bow to mild and affectionate means;
but it yielded under the hammer of adversity. His spirit was
made to bend to his father's will by that means; and, bending
home, he came to his father's house."[10]

The words of Alma contain an important insight concerning adversity. Surely it was not only Jesus who needed to
know "according to the flesh how to succor his people according to their infirmities" (Alma 7:11–12). All the rest of us
are expected to succor others at our lower level. But can we
have real empathy without experiencing some adversity? Can
we expect to be total strangers to suffering if we expect to be
fully understanding friends to others in their affliction?

In any case, we don't have to wait very long or go very far
before witnessing the appearance of adversity in life. The adversity is not solely physical. One might see a man with a very
painful and infected leg who, at that moment, is actually wor-
rying more over his simultaneous loss of status at the office.
We might encounter someone who is depressed but is also
suffering physically from a bleeding ulcer. We can suffer on
our comparatively small scale "both body and spirit"—interactive pain, both physical and mental anguish.

Since our fulness of joy will come only when purified body
and spirit are inseparably connected, could we appreciate that
later fulness of joy without first understanding and experiencing what happens when body and spirit are separated?

We may genuinely wonder if any good can come out of a particular situation of suffering. Whether the sufferer is actually growing and developing in some needed way may not be apparent to us. We may wonder whether the suffering of another person provides an opportunity for the rest of us for expressions of service, prayer, empathy, and attentiveness that we need to develop further.

In any case, we always need to remember that life is to be a proving experience for all, in which our faith and patience will be tried (Mosiah 23:21). God has so structured mortality, and there are no immunities.

We also need to remember that mortality is so structured that it rains on the just and the unjust alike (see Matthew 5:45). And as expressed earlier, there are certain afflictions "common to man" (1 Corinthians 10:13).

Meanwhile, we should not be worried if we cannot explain all things right now (see 1 Nephi 11:17).

What is desired is meekness, not glibness. Constant articulateness is not as vital as constant submissiveness.

These are hard but true doctrines! Be true to them.

I love you.
Grandfather

Notes

1. For all John Taylor references in this letter see *JD* 1:148.

2. *JD* 11:42.

3. PBS production of *The Good Soldier*, by Ford Maddox Ford, viewed in early 1983.

4. *JD* 2:301–2.

5. *JD* 11:174.

6. Brigham Young, *JD* 11:240.

7. *Teachings*, p. 216.

8. See also Brigham Young, *JD* 3:223.

9. *JD* 2:303.

10. *JD* 6:338.

Remembering Our Blessings

Dear Andrea:

Yes, we are so slow to remember some things and so quick to forget others! Your own appreciative ways made your comments on this matter authentic.

The flow of today's new worries can quickly dilute our appreciation of yesterday's blessings. Ancient Israel's appreciation for being rescued from too much water at the Red Sea (they even sang a commemorative song—see Exodus 15:1–19), soon gave way in Sinai to their complaints over too little water. Their immediate thirst obscured their remembrance of past blessings. More than we know or will admit, our spiritual staying power is clearly tied to our remembering.

Ironically, good times have a special way of inducing forgetfulness. Forgetfulness can be so relentless, even if it is not malicious. No wonder we sometimes need severe reminders: "And thus we see that except the Lord doth chasten his people with many afflictions, yea, except he doth visit them with death and with terror, and with famine and with all manner of pestilence, they will not remember him" (Helaman 12:3).

Furthermore, unless we are meek, past blessings may come to seem like an entitlement justifying fresh requests. We may be tempted to say, "What has God done for me lately." We expect fresh blessings even when these are not freshly deserved!

All the while we especially overlook certain basic blessings. We seldom count these blessings even though they count for so much. For instance, God lends us oxygen in order to breathe from moment to moment (see Mosiah 2:21). He provides a habitable planet (which we hope man will not destroy). Reverential remembering keeps us humble. I wonder how many testimonies have merely been forgotten?

How many, like Amulek, "knew concerning these things, yet
. . . would not know"? (Alma 10:6.)

Yet the gifts of all these basic blessings can come to be regarded as "givens." Their very repetitiveness creates a sense of
ordinariness.

We also get confused about causality, sometimes believing in the works of our own hands more than in God's handiwork: "And thou say in thine heart, My power and the might
of mine hand hath gotten me this wealth" (Deuteronomy
8:17).

You may rightly ask, "What are some of the remedies?"

1. "Give place" in our minds and schedules more often
   for pondering past blessings with their corrective perspective. Even three minutes of remembering will
   bring to mind many blessings. Loved ones and leaders
   can help us, too, by providing a longitudinal look:
   "Remember the days of old, consider the years of
   many generations: ask thy father, and he will shew
   thee; thy elders, and they will tell thee" (Deuteronomy 32:7). Our remembering can be part of our humbling. Dorothy Sayers said: "Pure religion has, in fact,
   a good deal in common with pure science. . . . What
   they have chiefly in common is humility."[1]

2. Reduce our Martha-like anxieties (see Luke
   10:28–32) over those urgent matters which are not
   automatically important just because they are urgent.
   As an illustration, the ringing phone may only be a
   recorded sales pitch. Short-term benefits are often
   taken from us or are quickly used up, anyway. So let's
   recognize many of the pressing things of the moment
   for what they really are.

3. Increase the number of our Mary-like choices, the
   benefits of which will not be taken from us. When a
   clear choice is placed before you, go for the long-
   term.

4. At least occasionally offer a prayer of pure thanksgiv-
   ing, without any petitions—at least for that moment,
   anyway!

5. Recognize that when endured well, certain deprivations increase our capacity for later appreciation.
6. Understand that being "added upon" by the experiences of the second estate is like remodeling and adding to our individual mortal house. The costs, pains, and frustrations of remodeling are real and may be resented. C. S. Lewis put it so well:

Imagine yourself as a living house. God comes in to rebuild that house. At first, perhaps, you can understand what He is doing. He is getting the drains right and stopping the leaks in the roof and so on: you knew that those jobs needed doing and so you are not surprised. But presently He starts knocking the house about in a way that hurts abominably and does not seem to make sense. What on earth is He up to? The explanation is that He is building quite a different house from the one you thought of—throwing out a new wing here, putting on an extra floor there, running up towers, making courtyards. You thought you were going to be made into a decent little cottage: but He is building a palace.[2]

With appreciation for your instinctive gratefulness.

Eternal love,
Grandfather

Notes

1. Quoted in *Around the Year with C. S. Lewis and His Friends*, Kathryn Lindskoog, comp. (Norwalk, Connecticut: C. R. Gibson Company, 1986), June 3. (Hereafter cited as *Around the Year.*)

2. C. S. Lewis, *Mere Christianity* (New York: Macmillan, 1943), p. 174.

Educating Our Desires

Dear Jacob:

How, you inquire, can we better "educate our desires," as President Joseph F. Smith urged?[1] Doing this is a tall order. So much could be said about it. However, since this is being written aloft in an airplane, and on a short flight, a few comments must suffice for now.

One little-used way of more honestly testing the correctness of our desires is to place those desires more honestly and specifically before God in reverent, personal prayer. Why so? Because if we are too embarrassed to petition Him concerning some of our desires, this will quickly confirm their incorrectness! Desires not worthy of our asking Him for help in achieving them are unworthy of us as well. Obviously, such desires should not be further nurtured in our hearts and minds.

Alas, some of us nurse certain desires secretly which would involve breaking God's commandments in some degree. Hence instead we pray to God over our "safe" agendum, rather than honestly asking Him for help in dismissing our dangerous desires. Since He knows of these errant, secret desires anyway, we ought to ask for His help in dismissing them.

Basically, however, we can educate our desires only as we learn more about what God's desires for us are. Since He is perfect in knowledge and love, we can trust Him to desire what is best for us—now and forever. This is part of coming to have the "mind of Christ," which facilitates our developing His desires within us (see 1 Corinthians 2:16).

Your enthusiasm for life and your basic goodness are so commendable. They always have been.

I love you.
Grandfather

Notes

1. See Joseph F. Smith, *Gospel Doctrine* (Salt Lake City: Deseret Book Company, 1966), p. 297.

Suffering's Developmental Role

Dear Heather:

You were apparently puzzled while hearing a Church leader speak about how suffering can be purifying.

To begin with, suffering certainly concentrates the mind, doesn't it? Suffering can also scrape off hindering encrustations of ego and error. Each of these effects can facilitate purification. Suffering can also bring about improved personal comprehending.

Even so, Elder John Taylor candidly observed, "So far as I am concerned, . . . I do not desire trials; I do not desire affliction. . . . I do not want to put a straw in anybody's way." However, he went on to say: "I used to think, if I were the Lord, I would not suffer people to be tried as they are; but I have changed my mind on that subject. Now I think I would, if I were the Lord, because it purges out the meanness and corruption that stick around the Saints, like flies around molasses."[1]

Another essential task is to "give away" whatever is left of our sins in order to know God (see Alma 22:18). All of this surely facilitates purifying.

Since, if we shrink from submission, we can't be "swallowed up in the will of God" (see Mosiah 15:7), suffering can help persuade us to yield, to surrender unconditionally to God, and to quit holding back. Each of these things purifies us and shrinks the distance between us and Him.

Therefore we appear to need certain clinical experiences involving adversity in order to help purify us spiritually. Just as food, water, and air are clearly essential to our physical survival, so the clinical experiences are necessary to make life developmentally meaningful. However, we certainly do not seek such tutorial experiences. In fact, we try to avoid them; we resist the spiritual equivalents of "Eat your spinach."

One can observe the developmental differences certain experiences make, especially over the years. Brigham Young could have remained as a conscientious craftsman and an upstanding local citizen in New England. He doubtless could have stayed there and made real contributions to his local community. Compare that outcome, however, to his having become (through his soul-stretching and developmental experiences) a modern Moses!

By the way, Brigham said that without the Restoration he would probably not have been much of a local churchman for want of doctrinal satisfaction. "Before I had made a profession of religion, I was thought to be an infidel by the Christians, because I could not believe their nonsense. The secret feeling of my heart was that I would be willing to crawl around the earth on my hands and knees, to see such a man as was Peter, Jeremiah, Moses, or any man that could tell me anything about God and heaven. . . . until I saw Joseph Smith."[2]

Eliza Snow might have remained in Ohio, writing occasional poems for the local paper, being a decent, good, serviceable local citizen. Instead, she became a poetess of a dispensation! In the exodus from Nauvoo, when she was bouncing along the frozen surface of Iowa "seated . . . on a chest, with a brass kettle and a soap box for our foot stools," she said she was "thankful" she "was so well off."[3] Could she have done that and all she later did, including leading the Relief Society once she was in the West, without the preceding enlarging experiences?

Notably, however, Jesus advised, "the spirit . . . is willing, but the flesh is weak" (Matthew 26:41). So it is that while we understand spiritually that we need clinical experiences, the natural man quite naturally flees from these; he misreads these trials.

President Brigham Young observed that

> people of the Most High God must be tried. It is written that they will be tried in all things, even as Abraham was tried. . . . Do not be discouraged when you hear of wars, and rumours of wars, and tumults, and contentions, and

fighting, and bloodshed; for behold they are at the thresholds of our doors. Now, do not let your hearts faint; for all this will promote the kingdom of God, and it will increase upon the earth. Why? Because the world will decrease. We will be strengthened, while they will be weakened.[4]

With admiration for your constancy in the things of the kingdom over the years, I love you.

Grandfather

P.S.

One weakness of the flesh is letting the mistakes of yesterday hold tomorrow hostage. Similarly, too much worry over the impending or imagined cares of tomorrow can fatigue us as we do the vital chores of today: "Sufficient unto the day . . ."

Notes

1. *JD* 5:114–15.
2. *JD* 8:228.
3. Kenneth W. Godfrey, et al., *Women's Voices* (Salt Lake City: Deseret Book Company, 1982), p. 147.
4. *JD* 4:369.

The Last Freedom

Dear Brittany:

How we handle life's little irritations often exposes how large our remaining selfishness is. Little irritations show, sometimes embarrassingly, the gap between what we know and what we are.

Often these little irritations are merely dressed-up versions of childish concerns over "my turf," "my praise," "my place," "my possessions," and "my timetable." We sometimes behave as if we were an irritated spider minding its web, sensitive to any disturbing vibrations and quick to move against any intruder.

It is seen in the simplest of daily things: The light is green, but the car ahead is not moving; he is in "my" way, holding "me" up!

How vital it is that we remember people's true identity as sons and daughters of God, along with remembering our own! The more we remember *who* we and others are, the less we will be vexed by the *what, how,* and *why* of things.

A valiant Jewish psychiatrist who had been confined in a Nazi concentration camp, Viktor E. Frankl, said "the last of human freedoms" is the ability to "choose one's attitude in a given set of circumstances."[1] Frankl believed that those having a "why" for living could bear any "how." The fulness of the gospel gives us so many "whys" but still leaves us free to choose our attitudes.

However, a wrong sense of worth, such as overmuch pride in our individual self and agency, celebrates what is the smallness of self. Only when set free by Jesus' truths is the small self emancipated out of the prison of pride. Only with knowing what we have the power to become is the losing of the old self correctly seen as no loss at all. Actually, the finding of the real self should bring the same rejoicing as in the return of the prodigal son.

In order for us to mount a successful rebellion against the natural man, meekness must lead the way. Only when the natural man is "put off" is the discovery of the real self possible. In the war for the soul, the enemy has seen to it that the truth about who we really are has been surrounded by "a bodyguard of lies," carefully deployed to prevent our discovery of the real self.

Jesus, who knew who He was, scrupulously avoided letting the little irritations reach Him. Big individuals refuse to be vexed by little irritations, which is yet another dimension of freedom.

Eternal love,
Grandfather

Notes

1. Viktor E. Frankl, *Man's Search for Meaning* (New York: Washington Square Press, 1985), p. 12.

Enlargement by Submission

Dear Sarah Jane:

We marvel at how well Jesus understood others, even while being misunderstood himself. He was able to think of the needs of others, while others neglected Him. He was able to nurture others, while He was suffering himself.

By being so totally unselfish, He was fully magnified. When we allow our will to be "swallowed up in the will of the Father" (Mosiah 15:7), then and only then do we "see things as they really are and as they really will be" (Jacob 4:13). Then we can learn things we "never had supposed" (Moses 1:10). When we are blessed with such perspective, what seems to be a sacrifice may be an opportunity or the gaining of experience which is for our good (D&C 122:7).

What the Lord is asking us to do is to see with His eyes, to think with His mind, and to feel with His heart. Those in the City of Enoch made their mark in this regard (see Moses 7:18). Though we cannot really do that to anything approaching a full degree, we can further trust Him by letting our will be further "swallowed up" in His. Among other things, doing this will greatly enlarge our empathy for others. To "put off the natural man" permits us to open our eyes, to enlarge our minds, and to enlarge our hearts.

Why do we resist? It seems as hard to let go of certain attitudes as it is to let go of goods and possessions. He wants us to restructure our understanding of reality. Was this not part of the prophet Benjamin's plea? "Believe in God; believe that he is, and that he created all things, both in heaven and in earth; believe that he has all wisdom, and all power, both in heaven and in earth; believe that man doth not comprehend all the things which the Lord can comprehend" (Mosiah 4:9).

Since we cannot see with His perfect eyes, think with His perfect mind, and feel with His perfect heart, our only alternative is to let our will be "swallowed up" in His as the way to access greater vision. Then we can receive, submissively, His direction and influence upon us. There is no other way.

Eternal love,
Grandfather

The Need for Nourishment

Dear Ashley:

Most of us fail to make adequate allowance for the steady erosion of daily life upon our faith and spiritual well-being. We can thereby so easily become "weary" and "faint in our minds" (see Hebrews 12:3). Daily life is so incessant and demanding; the cares of the world so pervasive and so constant, wearing down the best of us, *unless* we receive adequate and regular spiritual nourishment. This nourishment comes through study, service, worship, and prayer. In the warning words of Paul, "Wherefore let him that thinketh he standeth take heed lest he fall" (1 Corinthians 10:12).

Never wonder why we need the Spirit of the Lord to be with us, along with constant doctrinal nourishment, steady nurturing, regular association with the righteous, and along with the steadying and reminding duties, programs, and activities of the Church.

We simply are not good enough to make it alone! Moreover, succeeding spiritually ensures our not being alone!

Eternal love,
Grandfather

No Growth Without Discipline

Dear Lauren:

The fair-weather follower of Jesus naively wants discipleship without discipline. He wants soul enlargement, but without soul excavation. He will accept spiritual remodeling, but only if accomplished without real cost or serious inconvenience. If we thus expect erroneously, no wonder Deity will not respond when we petition amiss (see James 4:3; 2 Nephi 4:35).

When we willingly submit ourselves to God, even "as a child doth submit to his father" (Mosiah 3:19), we are not yielding just to any father but to a perfect Father! While it is a yielding, happy irony, one is thereby "added upon" (Abraham 3:26).

We are to yield our gifts and talents and not bury them. The duty of developing and sharing them, which you wondered about, has multiple levels of meaning. While God endows us each with certain gifts and talents, these still require of us much personal self-discipline. This is needed in order for us to develop and share these gifts fully.

God supplies the basic gift or talent, but it is we who are left to develop it, hone it, and share it. Then, He will give the increase. Rather than using the talent merely to please ourselves and to be owned possessively by us, let us share what God has so generously shared with us.

One may, for instance, have special physical skills or a great singing voice, which, with self-discipline and training, become highly developed. Often, however, the developer forgets the Giver, just as those who get rich may wrongly conclude, "my own hand hath gotten me this" (Deuteronomy 8:17).

Did the star athlete supply his own, original, special musculature? Did the renowned opera singer provide his own special vocal chords and lung capacity? Of some who were arrogant about their special status, Jesus once observed, "God is able of these stones to raise up children unto Abraham" (Matthew 3:9).

The test, therefore, is always what we "return" on the talents given to us. The yield is higher if we yield to God's purposes. Meekness helps us to remember whence the gifts came. If, instead, we are confused about causality, we invite pride to set the stage for the enactments and performances of ego.

With you, I admire high achievers who show genuine gratitude for their gifts even after their considerable diligence and self-discipline in developing and humbly sharing these gifts. Doing so is part of acknowledging and "confessing God's hand in all things," including the gifts His hand has so generously given to us (see D&C 59:21).

I love you,
Grandfather

Stand Firm Amid the Turmoil

Dear Grandchildren:

Over the years in my separate communications to you and in group discussions, perhaps I have not allowed sufficiently for the special convergence of trying conditions and vexing events in your time. These multiple "signs of the times" with their pervasive consequences are bound to affect your feelings about life.

Just to recite a few, you are aware of today's belching sensualism, rising terrorism, divisive nationalism, natural disasters, "distress of nations," and of "all things [being] in commotion" (D&C 88:91). We are even told a desolating scourge will one day go forth in the earth; and this will not be just a local plague (see D&C 5:19). Likewise, there will be a sifting in the Church, in order for it to become more sanctified as well as grow numerically (see 1 Nephi 14:12–14; D&C 105:31). Furthermore, we are told that conditions will be as in the days of Noah (see Matthew 24:37–38), including "violence" and "corruption" (Genesis 6:11).

Then, while in the midst of "all these things," you are asked to take up the cross daily while trusting in God, who has said, "I am able to do mine own work" (2 Nephi 27:21). He truly has "made ample provision"[1] for these conditions in the wickedness in the world. He will still bring to pass all His purposes. He has also assured us that, while we cannot bear all things now, we can further develop our bearing capacity. He will even make ways for us to escape certain things. He will be in our midst and lead us along. (See 1 Corinthians 10:13; D&C 78:18.)

Amid all this you will sense more keenly the real significance of daily discipleship. Even in the midst of converging challenges and sweeping events there is really never any greater challenge for a person than to keep his or her covenants. This achievement may seem rather "micro" amidst such "macro" events; yet daily cross carrying is the stuff of discipleship in any age (see Luke 9:23).

In his age, Lot was vexed by "filthy conversation" (2 Peter 2:7)—as many of us are vexed today, not only by filthy conversation but also by pornography on television, in music, and otherwise. As dramatic as the brave passage through the Red Sea was, those in our time who make their way through a sea of filth and still keep the seventh commandment will be even more victorious and deserving of praise.

We are told by some that we are in the post-Christian era. Unfortunately, though, we were never really in a Christian era. It is true, however, that more and more people no longer believe in the central Christian doctrines or in divinely given absolutes and rules.

Of the so-called post-Christian man, C. S. Lewis wrote: "This results from the apostasy of the great part of Europe from the Christian faith. Hence a worse state than the one we were in before we received the Faith. For no one returns from Christianity in the same state he was in before Christianity, but into a worse state: the difference between a pagan and an apostate is the difference between an unmarried woman and an adulteress. For faith perfects nature, but faith lost corrupts nature."[2]

Given the expressions concerning the post-Christian nature of the Western world, we begin to appreciate, more than in the past, the significance of the purposes of the Restoration. "And righteousness will I send down out of heaven; and truth will I send forth out of the earth, to bear testimony of mine Only Begotten; his resurrection from the dead; yea, and also the resurrection of all men; and righteousness and truth will I cause to sweep the earth as with a flood" (Moses 7:62).

To have fresh evidence restored and newly delegated apostolic authority given in order to bear testimony of Jesus and His resurrection and that of all men—indeed this is the only thing that could re-energize and re-invigorate the faith so lacking on the part of many in the world today.

Parallel symptoms feed on each other. Failing homes lead to failing schools and to failing individuals, and vice versa. In

more ways than we care to measure, permissiveness diminishes self-discipline, upon which, in turn, democracy and liberty finally depend. Liberty and licentiousness cannot walk
arm in arm for very long. So we will see societies in which
there are the forms of freedom but not the substance of citizenship. Just how long will separation of powers work in constitutional government if there is a critical mass of individuals
who lack such self-discipline or who crave power and abuse?

"Obedience to the unenforceable" is what permits free societies to operate. It is out of self-discipline and love that
needed volunteerism likewise comes. How many dollars
spent in drug rehabilitation might have gone to help the environment? Or how many unnecessary health costs might have
gone to improve schools and teachers' salaries? How much,
too, does the perplexity of nations actually reflect the growing uncertainty of individual values? How much of the "distress of nations" reflects the permissiveness of nations?

Why is it we do not see the obvious? The decline of the
family triggered the rise of so many compensatory institu-
tions and programs, which, however sincere, are always
falling short. Under-funding will be chronic in a society which
under-loves. We even see the growing inability of government
to perform its primary function: the safety and security of its
citizens. Why is it, too, that we can't see how willing "obedience to the unenforceable" includes a willingness to defer
gratification, which is a clear contributor to the fashioning of
the future—whether it concerns the national debt or preserving pre-parental health for the sake of later offspring?

Why is it we could not see that our blurred ability to distinguish right from wrong would lead to a lionization of some
undeserving public figures? As once in ancient Israel, more
and more, "every man [does] that which [is] right in his own
eyes" (Judges 21:25).

But enough of sweeping trends!

True, the major events of history are shared on a massive
scale. They form the large canvass upon which individual
events and choices are likewise played out. However, even
though one's individual drama is played out in the large canvass of sweeping social, political, economic, and military

events, we are each still especially accountable for what happens in our own small dramas. Esau and Jacob's reconciliation, as their caravans met in the desert, was dramatic and spiritually significant regardless of what was happening elsewhere in the desert. Their public reconciliation, however, was no more significant spiritually than the drama of one prodigal son running home to one anxious father or mother.

Noah's ark doubtless achieved local notoriety while under such lengthy construction—more than the brother of Jared's barges. Nephi's ship, however, was built on the lonely seashore somewhere in the Middle East. The spiritual significance in all three cases is the same. Prophets were obedient to the will of the Lord, and people were saved!

How are we to "cry peace" when peace has clearly been taken from the earth? How are we to build bridges amidst patterns of widening polarization?

We should cry peace, when there is no peace, for the same reason that we practice chastity and fidelity amid declining moral standards. Our individual life-styles cannot speak for all mankind, but we can surely make our own statement! We still seek to build bridges in the midst of widening polarization, because this is a dimension of keeping the second great commandment. We can put our pontoons in place for bridge building even if others are not so disposed, or even if events blow them away. Is it any harder than forgiving "seventy times seven"?

I love you—each and all.

Grandfather

Notes

1. *Teachings*, p. 220.

2. Quoted in *The Quotable C. S. Lewis*, Wayne Martindale and Jerry Root, eds. (Wheaton, Illinois: Tyndale Publications, 1989), p. 482.

Imponderables in Children's Development

Dear Michael:

I can remember visiting your elementary school many years ago on "Grandparents' Day." It was such a delightful experience to see you among your friends. How strikingly similar the children in your class seemed way back then! Though there were obvious individual variations, you were all the same age and approximately the same size. A close observer would have seen some emerging differences, but to the visitor you and your friends were much alike.

However, this seeming sameness didn't last long with you and your friends—any more than it did with me and mine so many years before. With all children, emerging differences in physical appearance and size are accompanied by more striking spiritual differences that soon emerge. Over the years, any spiritual gaps become more discernible.

When self meets life, marked differences soon begin to appear. Decisions are made; responses are given. We don't have to wait long for life's differentiating developmental experiences, do we?

How a person meets disappointment, success, adversity, prosperity, temptation, opportunity, praise, blame, wealth, poverty, power, and so forth, makes all the difference. Life's whipsaw experiences soon make apparent the extent of the spiritual luggage we brought with us from the premortal estate—along with the other differences which flow from genes and from living in a particular family or home. Some of the children who sat in your classroom may have been very carefully nurtured at home, while others may have been somewhat neglected. Some may have been spoiled, while others were being disadvantaged.

Yet you all once sat together in an elementary classroom

with little knowledge of what trials and opportunities lay ahead. Ere long you will all be located as if on a spiritual scattergram. What were just a few points of initial difference on the spiritual compass, back in an elementary school, will eventually create vast differences in later destinations. Children may be given "the same instruction and the same information," yet it is "strange" to see the differences that emerge as between devotion and dissent (Alma 47:36).

Speaking of us all, the early confidence a parent might have in one child may be dissolved in deep disappointment. What seemed to be apparent goodness turned out to be only superficial. Other children seem to have "bad breaks"; if only they had had a better peer group, and so on. Some who looked much less promising blossom surprisingly. Others summon up previously unnoticed spiritual reserves and impressively overcome the world.

We are so soon separated, it seems, by the experiences of life!

Fortunately, a just and merciful God will take all the variables into account, including bad breaks, in ways that we could not possibly manage.

I love you.
Grandfather

P.S.

Good parents want their children to be better than they themselves are. Brigham Young said: "I wish the daughters of Israel to far exceed their mothers in wisdom. And I wish these young men and boys to far exceed their fathers. I wish my sons to far exceed me in goodness and virtue. This is my earnest desire concerning my children." And again: "The youth around me, in their addresses this day, have eulogized the life and ability of brother Brigham; I want you not only to do as I have done, but a great deal better."[1]

Notes

1. *JD* 2:17, 19.

Opposition and Murphy's Law

Dear Emily:

Yes, "Murphy's Law" may be considered as an irritating subset of "It must needs be, that there is an opposition in all things" (2 Nephi 2:11). This pattern of perversity is sometimes like a peacock which displays itself for no apparent reason. George Will described his "Ohio in 1895 Theory of History," founded on the fact that in Ohio in 1895 there were just two automobiles—and they collided![1]

God's plan does not preclude the presence of perturbations. In fact, we are told to plan on them!

I love you.
Grandpa

Notes

1. *The American Scholar, Autumn 1991,* p. 503.

To Speak or Not to Speak?

Dear Timothy:

Why, you ask, don't we differentiate more wisely between those moments when silence is the best response and those moments when the sword of truth should be drawn to flash above the foe?

Basically it is because we don't sufficiently trust the Lord for guidance in that moment. He could either help us to express silence or give us the needed voice. Instead we usually go with the instincts of the natural man, and that person vacillates between cowardice and expressions of ego.

It takes faith, meekness, and courage to say what needs to be said in the right way and at the right time, especially when we are not sure beforehand what the response of others will be. When facing such moments it is understandable that we yearn to see the end from the beginning.

To be wisely silent when we so much wish to be heard is a triumph of meekness over eagerness. Meek Jesus taught us, too, by His sermons of silence (see Matthew 27:14; 15:23; Luke 23:8–9). For the natural man, however, assertion is a validation of self: "I assert, so I am!"

On the one hand, how we yearn at times for someone to step forward boldly in order to rally the reluctant! Sometimes, however, to be silent is equally appropriate; others may already have said what needs to be said, and said it better! A wise pause can help us to ripen our later comments and keep us from uttering words we would gladly recall later on. Similarly, to listen in order to achieve a deeper understanding is a blessing in itself.

An important role we are frequently called upon to play is as an appreciative audience for others. Sometimes we are too busy to be about this underrated and less glamorous portion of our Father's business. There are never enough listeners!

Being part of an appreciative audience isn't just for supportive grandparents.

For what it is worth, though there are troublesome memories of moments when I should have spoken up, there are more stinging memories of moments when I should have been silent.

I know you will honor your parents by serving them, as they have served you.

I love you.
Grandfather

Real Status Endures

Dear Elizabeth:

Loss of status, formal or informal, can be hard indeed. Few of us tolerate it well. We are not sufficiently meek.

One often overlooked but instructive good example is John the Baptist. He had labored diligently and had gathered a significant following. Furthermore, even though John had done no miracle, no greater prophet, said the Lord of the prophets, had been born of woman than John the Baptist! (See Luke 7:28.)

Then Jesus came on the scene. Meekly recognizing His supremacy, John said, "He must increase, but I must decrease" (John 3:30).

How different John the Baptist was from those described in this verse: "And if any man shall seek to build up himself, and seeketh not my counsel, he shall have no power, and his folly shall be made manifest" (D&C 136:19).

Ego is so clever that it can persuade us we are serving a higher purpose by not being lowly! We are bound to notice offenses to ego, but what we do next, after we have noticed, is the real test.

There are inevitable adjustments and fluctuations in the size of our own formal circles of status or influence. However, there need never be a shrinkage in the circles of our spiritual significance if we are in the process of becoming men and women of Christ.

There is yet another lesson tucked away in the John the Baptist episode. Having done the courageous, right, and meek thing, nevertheless he sought reassurance somewhat later. Imprisoned, he inquired about the work—"should we look for another?"—by sending his disciples to inquire of Jesus (Luke 7:19–23.) Christ carefully reassured John, who once had been at the center of things but who now apparently felt left out.

Almost all of us know what it is like to feel left out. Yet we are always within God's circle of concern! Blessed are the meek, for they are not so dependent on the praise of men. The meek know who they really are, and their real and lasting status will prevail.

Mortal monuments, however pretentious, and the passing praise of the world, however lavish, do not really and finally matter. Meanwhile, princes come and go, just as in Shelley's "Ozymandias":

> . . . Two vast and trunkless legs of stone
> Stand in the desert. Near them, on the sand,
> Half sunk, a shattered visage lies, . . .
> . . . .
> And on the pedestal, these words appear:
> My name is Ozymandias, King of Kings,
> Look on my works, ye Mighty, and despair!"
> Nothing beside remains. Round the decay
> Of that colossal wreck, boundless and bare,
> The lone and level sands stretch far away.[1]

Blessings on you for being true to what is right. Hold fast, and one day you will be held fast in the welcoming arms of Jesus (see Mormon 5:11).

Your modesty is commendable. We often forget that our immodesty can enflame envy in another, even if the arson is unintended.

Eternal love,
Grandfather

P.S.

Modesty also helps us to be patient in the ebbs and flows of life. This is a part of having faith in our Heavenly Father. Actually, when we are unduly impatient we are suggesting we know what is best. Better than does God. Or, at least, we are asserting that our timetable looks better than His. Either way, we are immodestly questioning the reality of God's omniscience, aren't we?

Notes

1. *The Complete Poetical Works of Shelley* (Boston: Houghton Mifflin Co., 1901), p. 356.

When Correct Principles Seem to Compete

Dear Martha:

We are all "compassed about" with so many opportunities to learn and to serve; it illustrates somewhat differently the familiar "here a little, there a little" pattern (see D&C 128:21).

We need experience in applying the variety of correct principles to such a variety of life's situations. Take, for instance, the need to "speak the truth in love" (Ephesians 4:15). How does one do this, for instance, when others are very untruthful and unloving? Or when others may construe any moderation or conciliation by us as a sign of weakness? There are situations, too, when instead of speaking out in love we should hold back our own commentary; this also as an expression of love.

How could we possibly learn in the abstract to balance such considerations? In actual, personal experience, striving to be under the influence of the Spirit is crucial. Yet too often we do not have the Spirit with us. Why? Elder Erastus Snow observed: "If our spirits are inclined to be stiff and refractory, and we desire continually the gratification of our own will to the extent that this feeling prevails in us, the Spirit of the Lord is held at a distance from us; or, in other words, the Father withholds his Spirit from us in proportion as we desire the gratification of our own will. We interpose a barrier between us and our Father, that he cannot, consistently with himself, move upon us so as to control our actions."[1]

We usually are too busy pleasing ourselves without weighing consequences. Such choices bring consequences—intended and unintended, wanted and unwanted. These can teach us much, if we can learn from those experiences.

Yet since we all make mistakes, it is crucial that we not remain immobilized thereby. Otherwise we will find ourselves caught in a ritual of regret, as memory serves up "instant replays." Instead, part of repenting, in the broadest and most progressive sense of the word, is to move on! After corrective action it's hand to the plow, not looking back. Though we may have erred at the time because we lacked the Spirit, later the Spirit can help us learn from our mistakes.

All of this is admittedly much more easily said than done. But progressive repentance is achieved by many. Besides, applying a correct principle does not become any easier through procrastination.

Are there times when correct principles seem almost to be competing? Yes!

The narrowness of the straight and narrow way involves achieving a balance between tugging yet correct principles. Usually we cite the balancing of justice and mercy. But meekness and judgment likewise qualify as needing balanced interplay. Gospel principles are not opposites at all, yet they do require the unequalled synchronization of the Spirit. Balance on the straight and narrow path is crucial. Orthodoxy brings felicity. G. K. Chesterton wrote of "huge blunders" in human happiness caused by a lack of spiritual balance between tugging principles. "This is the thrilling romance of Orthodoxy. People have fallen into a foolish habit of speaking of Orthodoxy as something heavy, humdrum, and safe. There never was anything so perilous and so exciting as orthodoxy. It was sanity: and to be sane is more dramatic than to be mad."

Chesterton speaks of this "duplex passion," and of how modesty, for instance, is the balance between pride and prostration, of how courage, likewise, involves "a strong desire to live, taking the form of a readiness to die."[2]

Christ has all the celestial qualities in perfect balance. Working out our salvation includes developing the Christlike virtues and, likewise, knowing when and how to apply them.

Experience is such a vital teacher! For example, when does speaking the truth in love leave off, so that another's moral agency is finally recognized? How much loving pres-

sure can we properly and wisely apply? Oh, how we need the
synchronization of the Spirit!

Eternal love,
Grandfather

Notes

1. *JD* 7:352.
2. G.K. Chesterton, *Orthodoxy* (Garden City, New York: Image Books, 1959),
pp. 93, 100.

The Real Knowledge Explosion

Dear Lindsey:

Wisely, you have apparently wondered over the vexing challenge of sorting out from all the rest the things that really matter. The Spirit is the discerner, and conscience the sharp compass. So the sorting best occurs, and we help the process greatly, if we pause more often to ponder.

In life, not only do things come at us quickly but also the task is made even more vexing because each day we must make our way through the thick underbrush of the unimportant. Sometimes the refreshing meadows of the meaningful seem so occasional.

You mention the knowledge explosion, which has been useful in many ways. Yet so far as the salvation of souls is concerned, the secular knowledge explosion has not been a bang at all—merely a whimper of wisdom.

In terms of salvation, the real knowledge explosion in our time came through the Restoration, which put all things in true and precious perspective. One day this saving knowledge will cover the earth, being available to all who desire it (Moses 7:62). Part of this "roll out" will occur during the Millennium. Wickedness will clearly constrain the growth of the kingdom (see 1 Nephi 14:12).

It is so easy to end up "ever learning"—knowing more and more about less and less that matters, while failing to come to "the knowledge of the truth" of "things as they really are, and . . . as they really will be" (2 Timothy 3:7; Jacob 4:13). Christ's disciples should ever realize that in the underbrush of the unimportant or in the forest of facts there are many "who are only kept from the truth because they know not where to find it" (D&C 123:12). In our passion for equality we sometimes wrongly assume there is a democracy among truths.

Already, the Lord assures us, He and the shining light of
His restored gospel "cannot be hid" (D&C 14:9). His light
will not be extinguished, but instead it will grow "brighter
and brighter until the perfect day" (D&C 50:24). Elder
George Q. Cannon said it was too late even in 1860 for those
who would snuff out the kingdom:

> In our expulsion from Illinois, our journeyings across the
> Plains, our settlement in this Valley, all has contributed to
> make us what we now are. Our enemies see this, and they
> regret that they did not leave us to be mixed up with the
> world, so that civilization might have surrounded us, and
> its surges eventually have destroyed our organization. But
> we are here, and it is now too late. We are now estab-
> lished, and we have become a fixed power; we are grow-
> ing here in the mountains, and are beginning to be ac-
> knowledged and called a nation in the midst of the earth,
> and everything that the wicked have done and will do will
> be a source of regret to them, because they will see, as
> they have already seen, that they have worked into our
> hands.[1]

This last dispensation will be so unlike the time when the
Light of the World shined in the darkness of the meridian of
time and was not comprehended (see D&C 6:21). When He
comes to reign in majesty and power "all flesh shall see
[Him] together" (D&C 101:23; 88:93, 95; see also Matthew
24:30). Eventually and millennially, gospel standards will
even become the freely accepted standards for the nations
(D&C 14:9; 115:5).

However, back to your observation about our need for
perspective. It is the very lack of perspective which causes us
to "covet the drop" and to neglect the more weighty matters
(see D&C 117:8). Things which seem so significant and lasting can actually be so minuscule and transitory. "Behold, the
nations are as a drop of a bucket, and are counted as the
small dust of the balance: behold, he taketh up the isles as a
very little thing" (Isaiah 40:15).

Proud mortal lawmakers need to be aware that "ye shall

have no laws but my laws when I come, for I am your law-giver, and what can stay my hand?" (D&C 38:22).

Brigham Young taught, however, that in the Millennium there will still be intellectual and denominational diversity. "When all nations are so subdued to Jesus that every knee shall bow and every tongue confess, there will still be millions on the earth who will not believe in him; but they will be obliged to acknowledge his kingly government."[2]

However, there will at least be enough consensus then to provide a welcome world of terrestrial standards. What an immense relief!

With appreciation for your gladness in goodness.

Much love,
Grandfather

Notes

1. *JD* 8:303–4.
2. *JD* 7:142.

Abilities and Opportunities

Dear Erik:

The other night at the Grandchildren's Fireside your conversation reflected your increasing interest in things political. You wondered aloud about the frequent mismatch of individuals' abilities and their opportunities. They don't always correlate, do they? As in life generally, some individuals have more to offer than current circumstances seem able to absorb, others less than the opportunities permit. Most of us, however, live well below our available opportunities and privileges.

When there is a "match," truly great individuals are meek enough to recognize that events and circumstances permit them to display their leadership as well as to acknowledge the contributions of others.

Several years after World War II, Winston Churchill said: "I have never accepted what many people have kindly said, namely that I inspired the nation. . . . It was the nation and the race dwelling all round the globe that had the lion's heart. I had the luck to be called upon to give the roar!"[1]

Another British prime minister, however, had a different experience. "It was not the turn of any tide that began to upset the Prime Minister. What he had to face instead was the embarrassment of a tide at its flood. It was on the crest of his own wave that he was carried splendidly aloft but helpless amid the froth and foam of the enthusiasm of his admirers. He who wanted to lead was pushed. . . . one of those strokes of luck which, like a too vigorous slap on the back, leaves a man staggering."[2]

Events can be "controlling." Examples, if plotted, would result in a scattergram showing the varied interplay of *ability* and *opportunity*. More important, so many of us handle the prerogatives of power poorly when these opportunities come (see D&C 121:39). Few handle power well, but at certain critical junctures men and women truly have been raised up who possessed the wisdom and meekness to bless large numbers of people.

George Washington—the man who would *not* be king— was one of those "few men." "In all history, few men who possessed unassailable power have used that power so gently and self-effacingly for what their best instincts told them was the welfare of their neighbors and all mankind."[3]

The possessors of secular power have often allowed their intense loyalty to others to grind down their integrity. The tendency to indulge one's friends, or the failure to see betrayal or toadying sycophancy in their earliest stages, contribute to tragedy. "He that walketh with wise men shall be wise: but a companion of fools shall be destroyed" (Proverbs 13:20). Some political leaders have difficulty in personally discharging those who must go. Other leaders are too quick to provide scapegoats.

Another example for your files: Britain's Prime Minister Clement Attlee, for instance, sought to place lively individuals about him:

> The fatal mistake in making appointments was to select "docile yes-men." To guard against this Attlee sometimes chose to "put in people who are likely to be awkward." These were always to be warned in advance: "If you don't turn out all right I shall sack you." . . . And he was as good as his word.
>
> One junior minister . . . was summoned precipitously to Number ten, to be congratulated on the work of his department, he thought. "What can I do for you, Prime Minister?" he said, as he sat down. "I want your job," said Attlee. The minister was staggered. "But . . . why, Prime Minister?" "Afraid you're not up to it," said Attlee. The interview was over.[4]

Too often mortal power, status, acclaim, and riches are allowed to define people and their roles. How slowly, therefore, do some relinquish those trappings! Prime Minister

Neville Chamberlain, critics said, clung to power and office like a limpet.[5]

If only all of us understood our true and lasting identity and were not so dependent on fleeting things!

By the way, one of the great moments of reproof occurred in the parliament that marked the beginning of the end of Neville Chamberlain's prime ministership. There had been an immense buildup of frustration. On this occasion Parliament was packed, as various members began to attack Chamberlain's faltering administration. Leo Amery, the next speaker, quoted some lines from Oliver Cromwell on the need for fighting spirit and resolution. Then, to the rapt attention of Parliament, he added:

> I have quoted certain words of Oliver Cromwell. I will quote certain other words. I do it with great reluctance because I am speaking of those who are old friends and associates of mine, but they are words which, I think, are applicable to the present situation. This is what Cromwell said to the long Parliament when he thought it was no longer fit to conduct the affairs of the nation:
>
> "You have sat too long here from any good you have been doing. Depart, I say, and let us have done with you. In the name of God, go."[6]

It was a most dramatic moment and one that shattered Chamberlain.

Some who partake of power and praise come to depend upon such. They also find themselves addicted to it, "needing acclaim as a man with a goiter needs iodine."[7]

I offer this caution about biographies, much as I enjoy good ones: most "biographies are but the clothes and buttons of the man—the biography of the man himself cannot be written."[8]

One thing which political history makes clear is that in the political process we elect the whole individual—including his attitudes, habits, and tendencies. Granted, some of these are more directly relevant to the carrying out of his duties than others, but character, or the lack of it, will soon become evident.

Mussolini took away freedom, though he "made the trains run on time." Another dictator may achieve full employment, but only by building a great war machine. Much as we admire punctuality and desire full employment, certainly other criteria must be brought to bear. Therefore we cannot naively expect to separate the character of an individual who governs from how he governs.

It is not enough to say that Herod's lusting after Salome's dancing was merely a private thing. It cost John the Baptist his head! If an individual lies, that flaw in his character makes him vulnerable, because the lying will not automatically stop at the edge of public policy. A person who bears false witness should not ask us to be unconcerned as long as his practice of bearing false witness occurs only in private conversations.

Of course, all make mistakes and have the privilege of repenting. Of course, we should be merciful to each other, but not by setting aside God's relevant standards given Moses on Mount Sinai.

We cannot be consistent if we are concerned with damages to nature, our physical environment (even requiring businesses and corporations to provide an environmental impact study beforehand), and yet are unconcerned about the environment of human nature, including human relationships.

We may ask whether there is no terrain which is private? The answer is that there are no indoor and outdoor sets of the Ten Commandments!

Happily, however, we can function with some degree of effectiveness in some things, even though we are imperfect. Frankly, even while one is ignoring certain commandments, other existing virtues can apply: "And he did do justice unto the people, but not unto himself because of his many whoredoms; wherefore he was cut off from the presence of the Lord" (Ether 10:11).

However, leaders of a whole people should seek to have a wholeness of character, so that all, including themselves, might profit thereby.

No wonder we should all rejoice when integrity, ability,

and opportunity converge, so that the "wise," "good," and "honest" can serve people and causes well (see D&C 98:10). But power is risky, as section 121 of the Doctrine and Covenants makes soberingly clear. Misused, it not only can diminish an entire democracy but it can also diminish us individually.

Thanks for your own meek example over the years in the face of your impressive abilities—athletically and academically.

Much love,
Grandfather

Notes

1. Jack House, comp., *Winston Churchill: His Wit and Wisdom* (Hyperion Books, n.d.), p. 26.

2. P.W. Wilson, *William Pitt, the Younger* (Garden City: Doubleday, Doran & Company, 1930), p. 231.

3. James Thomas Flexner, *Washington the Indispensable Man* (New York: Plume, 1984), p. xvi.

4. Kenneth Harris, *Attlee* (London: Weidenfeld and Nicolson, 1982), pp. 406–7.

5. See William Manchester, *The Last Lion, Winston Spencer Churchill: Alone 1932–1940* (Boston: Little, Brown and Company, 1988), p. 665.

6. *The Last Lion*, pp. 654–55.

7. Ted Morgan, *Churchill, Young Man in a Hurry* (New York: Simon and Schuster, 1982), p. 434.

8. Mark Twain as quoted in *Around the Year*, July 16.

Our Many-Faceted Experiences

Dear Ryan:

They were clever comments you made the other night about how trials may seem to flow as if out of a fire hydrant. How, indeed, does one partake of them?

Experiences are seemingly so arranged as to provide multiple-use, clinical material. Several of us, if meek, may learn from the same episode—rather like spokes radiating from one hub. In addition, multiple things may be learned by a single individual from a single experience.

Yet our provincialism and self-centeredness can cause us to see only our particular facet of what may be a many-faceted, developmental diamond. This is like the situation in which our anxious eyes search the airport departure screen; we are looking for only one flight, yet there are numerous flights coming and going that involve many others just as important as we. This close-focused search is practical and understandable in an airport lounge, but as a life-style it is lamentable.

This is where the Lord's micro-management comes in, even though He honors our individual moral agency. Since there are countless considerations which only He knows, our patience with various situations is needed to complement God's longsuffering toward us. Otherwise we end up asking Him to please move things along so far as we are concerned, as if only one spiritual "flight" were involved.

A few years back, before you did as well academically, your loving parents had the challenge of balancing patience and admonition. You must have been frustrated at times, too. Yet they persisted, and so did you. Your mutual love was lubricant. You sensed that they really believed you could do better.

They were right!

With loving commendation,
Grandfather

The "Thou Shalt Nots"

Dear Brittany:

Given your typically positive attitude, it is unsurprising to have you ask why eight of the Ten Commandments are in the form of a "Thou shalt not." Only two are couched in a "Thou shalt."

Actually, the two commandments Jesus designated as the great commandments on which *all* others hang are profoundly positive: to love God with all our heart and to love our neighbors as ourselves (see Matthew 22:37–40).

At first, however, the "Thou shalt nots" sound sternly prohibitive, don't they? Yet so many of us have had to learn "by sad experience" (D&C 121:39). There are many paths to misery but only one to everlasting happiness. Even so, as Roger Keller has pointed out, while we certainly need this "interim list" of prohibitions now, with later spiritual maturity our obedience to "the divine will" becomes "instinctive."[1]

Furthermore, the two positive and great commandments can scarcely be kept if we are breaking the "Thou shalt not" commandments. How can we truly love God if we profane His name? Misuse His holy day? Abuse His children? Or let those in need pass by unnoticed? (See Mormon 8:39.) Likewise, how can we genuinely love our neighbors if we bear false witness against them? Even cynical and sarcastic humor breaches not only the first but the second great commandment as well. From time to time we all come to know some verbal abuse, including chatter from insensitive tongues. George MacDonald said: "Let a man do right, nor trouble himself about worthless opinion; the less he heeds tongues, the less difficult he will find it to love men."[2] This quote reminds us of a new play on old words: "Time wounds all heels."

Each day life's digressions and temptations are constant,

subtle, and specific. We have numerous chances to lie a little, covet a little, cheat a little, profane a little, gossip a little, be a little unforgiving, put someone down a little. Such temptations arise naturally in the daily course of things and are warmly welcomed by the natural man and woman. Therefore, since the ways in which we can transgress are so numerous and specific, so also are the matching "Thou shalt nots." Even so, "I cannot tell you all the things whereby ye may commit sin; for there are divers ways and means, even so many that I cannot number them" (Mosiah 4:29).

It is of little use, therefore, to speak of "what manner of men [and women we] ought to be," if we cannot successfully manage the specific and diverting temptations of daily life (3 Nephi 27:27; see also 2 Peter 3:11).

Remember, as far as the scope of good choices was concerned, it was of only one tree in the garden that Adam and Eve were *not* to partake. They could have partaken of many other fruits. Just so, we can "do many things" and be engaged in many good causes. We are not hedged in: "Verily I say, men should be anxiously engaged in a good cause, and do many things of their own free will, and bring to pass much righteousness; for the power is in them, wherein they are agents unto themselves. And inasmuch as men do good they shall in nowise lose their reward." (D&C 58:27–28.)

Seemingly small efforts finally accumulate to produce major good works.

Still, the danger zones need to be staked out, especially since "despair cometh because of iniquity" (Moroni 10:22). The constraining commandments are designed to keep us from despair and well inside the zone of happiness. Hence the need for restraining guardrails along the straight and narrow path.

Particularly in the last days, iniquity will bring about a diminished supply of love for others—just as Jesus prophesied (see Joseph Smith—Matthew 1:10; Matthew 24:12). Among many, the capacity to love will truly "wax cold," not merely "wax *lukewarm*."

Yet the impressions sometimes created by our enunciation and re-enunciation of all the specific prohibitions can make such repetition into an irritation, if we are not meek. These warnings may resemble the ever-present signs like No Diving in the Shallow End of the Pool, or, in hotel bathrooms, Please Put the Shower Curtain *Inside* the Tub. We shouldn't need such signs, but some do.

God's prohibitions also are linked to His divine developmental purposes for us. The prohibitive commandments allow us to measure ourselves more easily and specifically and are more easily kept, in a sense, whereas obeying the commandment "Love thy neighbor" is the work of a lifetime.

God desires that we be happy here, but especially that we also come home to Him. Hence the necessary blend of positive and negative commandments.

Another example of how the Lord teaches not only positively but also diagnostically was described well by Bishop Henry B. Eyring as he used this next example so effectively: When the brother of Jared was trying to build a vessel to cross the ocean, the Lord did not tell him exactly how to do everything down to the minutest detail, including how to provide the much-needed light. Instead, instructively and diagnostically, the Lord observed that the brother of Jared couldn't use fire or windows. These proscriptions provided certain parameters, but the brother of Jared developed his own inspired and affirmative solution to the vexing problem of providing light, and the Lord concurred. (See Ether 2:23; 3:4.)

Yes, a wise disciple will not dive in the shallow end of a swimming pool, and he will dutifully "put the shower curtain inside the tub." So many of us, however, need the reminders!

There are deeper considerations, of course, underlying the positive commandments. Certain attributes are required of the truly faithful as well as actions (see Mosiah 3:19). The quality of charity, for example, is central not only to keeping the great and affirmative first and second commandments but to all other commandments as well. A relevant and insightful quote from Brigham Young comes to mind: "There is one virtue, attribute, or principle, which, if cherished and practiced by the Saints, would prove salvation to thousands upon thousands. I allude to charity, or love, from which proceed forgiveness, long-suffering, kindness, and patience."[3]

Truly our capacity to love determines the degree to which we can develop all the other crucial qualities. Without love, we will be impatient. Without love, we will be unforgiving. Without love, we will be unkind and unmerciful. Brigham Young was right on, once again!

> Your loving Grandfather, who admires your blend of brightness and instinctive goodness.

P.S.

Because of your own creativity, these lines from Rudyard Kipling will likely please you as they anticipate a distant day:

> When Earth's last picture is painted
> and tubes are twisted and dried,
> When the oldest colours have faded,
> and the youngest critic has died,
> We shall rest, and, faith, we shall need it—
> lie down for an aeon or two,
> Till the Master of All Good Workmen
> Shall put us to work anew.
>
> . . . .
>
> And only the Master shall praise us,
> and only the Master shall blame;
> And no one shall work for money,
> and no one shall work for fame,
> But each for the joy of the working,
> and each, in his separate star,
> Shall draw the Thing as he sees It
> for the God of Things as They are![4]

Notes

1. Foundation for Ancient Research and Mormon Studies (FARMS) paper "Laws and Commandments in the Book of Mormon," 1991, pp. 16–17.

2. Quoted in *Around the Year*, March 7.

3. *JD* 7:133–34.

4. From "L' Envoi," in Roy J. Cook, comp. *One Hundred and One Famous Poems* (Chicago: The Reilly & Lee Co., 1958),. p. 172.

The Heart Must Be Engaged

Dear Robbie:

Yes, God is a God of law. This sounds stern, but first and last He is a perfect Father of loving-kindness. For example, even though we do not have our lives fully in order, when we obey *some* laws we receive some blessings (see D&C 130:21). It is all part of God's loving fairness. Significantly, those who devotedly follow "the commandments of men" can still experience a diverting success and "joy for a season" (see 3 Nephi 27:11). But their joy is not deep and lasting.

At the same time, adequate outward performance may mask grave inward deficiencies. The Old Testament ruler, Amaziah, "did that which was right in the sight of the Lord," but it was not done with a perfect heart (2 Chronicles 25:2). Unsurprisingly, he soon faltered. Having real intent of heart and heeding spiritual memory combine to provide us with the needed staying power.

Strange as it seems, some are more fair to others than they are to themselves! Morianton, for instance, was able to prosper a whole nation he had conquered with an army of outcasts. Furthermore, as a ruler he dealt justly with his people. However, he was not fair with himself. In what way? Because of his immoral life-style. He was his own victim! (See Ether 10:11.)

When we sin, we not only sin against God and others but also we actually sin against ourselves. We act against our own self-interest, leaving self-inflicted wounds. Morianton would have done well to follow this sage advice: "You cannot play with the animal in you without becoming wholly animal, play with falsehood without forfeiting your right to truth, play with cruelty without losing your sensitivity of mind. He who wants to keep his garden tidy doesn't reserve a plot for weeds."[1]

Thanks for being interested enough to ask! With admiration for your self-discipline.

Eternal love,
Grandfather

Notes

1. Dag Hammarskjold, *Markings* (New York: Alfred A. Knopf, 1968), p. 14.

In Our Time and Place

Dear Jacob:

Like Alma, who wished for a trumpet-like voice of an angel (see Alma 29:1), we too need to understand our motivations and limitations. Even so, let us use well the season in which we serve. Tolkein put it eloquently: "Yet it is not our part to master all the tides of the world, but to do what is in us for the succor of those years wherein we are set, uprooting the evil in the fields that we know, so that those who live after may have clean earth to till. What weather they shall have is not ours to rule."[1]

Nephi wished, nostalgically, he'd lived in a different time, yet finally concluded, "But behold, I am consigned that these are my days" (Helaman 7:9). Like Alma, he no doubt realized that he should not "desire more than to perform the work to which [he had] been called" (Alma 29:6). Faith in God includes faith in His wisdom in placing us in our particular time and place, "those years wherein we are set."

At times, faith still leaves a poignant zone of perplexity and puzzlement as to just how much we can realistically strive to influence things affirmatively "in the fields that we know."

Our emerging "why" questions can help us, however, to develop greater faith in God's purposes for us in our time, because answers do come to most "why" questions.

Most important, however, whether in scope or depth, none of our "whys" even remotely approach in poignancy Jesus' "Why?" in His soul-rending "Why hast thou forsaken me?" (Mark 15:34.) Yet submissive, suffering Jesus nevertheless "finished His preparations unto the children of men" (see D&C 19:19).

Our "how long" questions, honestly asked, can help us to increase our *patience* with God's timing. Prophets have been involved in similar expressions and experiences in the midst of their deep anguish and puzzlement (see Jeremiah 20:9).

Since we walk by faith, not by sight (2 Corinthians 5:7), some puzzlement is likely, for we do not see the end from the beginning. If we constantly saw the end from the beginning, the "middle" would not be a true test! Therefore, it shouldn't surprise us that our individual experiences so often bear directly on developing our *faith* and *patience* (see Mosiah 23:21). In any case, how could those same two special qualities—both of which are eternal and portable—be further developed in the absence of the relevant experiences?

You also inquired about the difficulties of selecting among the various good causes. When we select causes it should be done with the same care prescribed for our seeking out those who lead us govermentally. The operative, revealed words are "wise," "good," and "honest" (D&C 98:10). To causes which so qualify, we may give our money, our time, our talent, or perhaps even lend our names. *Wise* causes qualify as being wise both in the short and the long term; they are truly cost-effective in their use of human and financial resources. They are *good* all the way through, not just cosmetically; they do not advance naive or false solutions which may contain within them new problems. *Honest* causes prevent those "anxiously engaged" from being wrongly manipulated and from endorsing that which is undeserving.

We surely can't respond to all good causes, but we can do some things, especially those things which relieve the human misery over which you are commendably concerned. Closest to home, we can do more to reduce any misery in our own lives, in our own families, in our own neighborhoods, and in our own communities. A duty rests upon the faithful: "We then that are strong ought to bear the infirmities of the weak, and not to please ourselves" (Romans 15:1).

Our "light may be a little one," but, as a wise man remarked, "A candle is not lighted for itself, and neither is a man." Candles are especially noticed in the darkness.

May you continue to light the way!

I love you.
Grandfather

Notes

1. J.R.R. Tolkein, *The Return of the King* (New York: Ballantine Books, 1955), p.190.

This Is It!

Dear Andrea:

Yes, amid daily life we may mistakenly think there is something more exotic or dramatic, beyond keeping God's commandments, which we are supposed to be doing. Instead, however, "this is it!"

To be sure, there are sometimes periodic and personalized chores along the way. Even so, all specialized chores are merely branches of keeping the first and second commandments, anyway. In eternal significance, nothing finally compares to the importance of keeping our covenants while taking up the cross daily (see Luke 9:23).

Furthermore, there are no blessings which exceed those that will be given to us if we keep our covenants, for after that we will receive "all that [the] Father hath" (D&C 84:38).

However, there may even be a few times when, underwhelmed, we might plead, "More used would I be" (*Hymns* no. 131). But the significance of the individual righteous life cannot be overstated.

In the course of things, we may not be able to avoid contemplating or anticipating something in a patriarchal blessing or wondering how a particular calling will unfold. But generally speaking we are picked up and carried along by the surf of events and circumstances of daily life. Remaining faithful while being thus tossed is both exhilarating and sobering. Even when we feel a little helpless in the surf of circumstances, we are still in His hands. He has foreseen the surf and its destination and velocity. The surf may even be of His making. If we've not been breathless or surprised for a while, it may be time again. Even so, He can likewise calm the raging seas lest we become too fearful.

You mentioned someone you admire, wondering aloud if she knows how special she is amid her particular surf of circumstances. She may not. I don't think our great President Spencer W. Kimball ever really knew how special he was. As for incoming compliments, his modesty was like a deflecting canopy.

Most of us will have had experience with someone who is already especially good but who is still growing visibly in spirituality. Such individuals seem only partially aware of their progress. This occurs because they are not always selfishly taking their own temperature but instead are busy serving and giving. It is their meekness! They are not preoccupied with themselves. We may mistakenly wonder if they are naive, but we soon come to realize that their goodness is not conscious of itself; it is too busy seeking small opportunities to bestow itself.

Progress on the pathways of discipleship is cumulative. "Therefore, a thousand acts, each in itself all but valueless, are of inestimable worth as the necessary and connected gradations of an infinite progress."[1] Such growth may "indicate a saint."

President Young said, "I wish the people not to lose sight of one thing: that every day's labor, every moment's toil, every prayer and exertion which they make points to the building up of the kingdom of God upon the earth."[2]

I love you.
Grandfather Neal

Notes

1. *MacDonald Anthology,* p. 3.
2. *JD* 10:19.

How to Treat a Wayward Friend

Dear Heather:

You ask just how far your responsibility extends as regards your friend who is misbehaving, thereby distancing herself from her family, the Church, and apparently even from you. It is so like you to be thoughtfully concerned.

One of life's toughest interpersonal challenges involves our tender concern for an offending friend who deserves reproof. Yet because of friendship we are reluctant to reprove, fearing that only further distance will develop. We fret over how to help, but unfortunately we often end up by not "interfering." It's a mistake I've made a few times.

A wider sense of proportion would sensitize us much more to the needs of those being offended as well as to those of the offender. The offended and their feelings matter too. These individuals, however, are sometimes under-represented as compared to our immediate and intense concerns for the offender. A sensitive inventory of all those being adversely affected might evoke a little more democracy of sympathy. Usually we resist reproving lovingly "early on," as the scriptural word *betimes* directs (see D&C 121:43). But we are not someone's enemy just because we tell him the truth.

We may rationalize that the offense is not too bad. We fear over-responding. We fear the offender's reactions. We hope it will all work out some other way. Perhaps someone else will deal with it.

Whatever the reasons, our fear of the offender's potential resentment can postpone his repentance, which, if achieved earlier, would have been much less costly to him. Furthermore, an early response might shorten the list of his "victims," whether of his bad temper or his greed.

It is certainly more popular to exhibit mercy than to apply justice, isn't it?

Just when an offender needs most to encounter justice by bumping up against restraining righteousness, we let him or her go unchallenged. Provocative one-liners might cause him to pause, if not to stop. Inwardly and unconsciously, he may even be hoping for restraint. Disapproving silence is usually no substitute for loving reproof.

President Brigham Young observed that it is "not pleasant to our feelings" to receive a rebuke. We may realize our error, but "we do not like to have anyone tell us" about our mistakes. In that same sermon President Young continued by saying he wished the members of the Church, "when they are rebuked by a friend, to receive that rebuke kindly, and kiss the rod, and reverence the hand that administers it—to learn that the rebuke of a friend is for our good." There are "degrees of chastisement." Some are slow to respond to reproof, he observed, whereas others have their hearts broken, because their feelings are "as an infant, and will melt like wax before the flames. . . . You must chasten according to the spirit that is in the person. Some you may talk to all day long, and they do not know what you are talking about. There is a great variety. Treat people as they are."[1]

Whatever the individual case, our task is to "continue to minister" without cynically computing the odds, "for unto such shall ye continue to minister; for ye know not but what they will return and repent, and come unto me with full purpose of heart, and I shall heal them; and ye shall be the means of bringing salvation unto them" (3 Nephi 18:32).

Of course, the determined offenders may ignore even our best efforts. Being "free to choose" for themselves, they may crash through all reproof and restraint. Nevertheless, in our sometimes collective failure to try at all, we all fail. Then we gather solemnly at the foot of the cliff, hoping to salvage something from the smoking, twisted human wreckage. Instead we might have been loving, restraining sentries atop the cliff, or workers called upon to oversee, repair, and replace the guardrails.

You will be blessed to know how to proceed. Your love may not be reciprocated, but it will not be wasted. Don't fret over possible clumsiness on your part. Real love is felt even when it is poorly expressed. Furthermore, if we "[show] forth afterward an increase of love" (D&C 121:43) we will more likely be seen as a true friend and not an enemy.

Never forget Jesus' encouragement and direction: "Moreover if thy brother shall trespass against thee, go and tell him his fault between thee and him alone: if he shall hear thee, thou hast gained thy brother" (Matthew 18:15). No one is finally lost until we give up!

May you "gain" back your friend. Mind the moment, and eternity will take care of itself.

Your loving Grandfather

Notes

1. JD 8:364–67.

Bold and Never Boring

Dear Sarah Jane:

Early members of the Church, with all their journeys, re-locations, and persecutions, didn't have much leisure time in which to study the Book of Mormon in great detail. Nevertheless they received a firm testimony of its authenticity.

This fact is symbolized by a few surviving tombstones in southern Ohio and Indiana which speak for themselves. Displayed atop those tombstones are a stone Bible and Book of Mormon. Those early members left evidence that they knew, through the Restoration, we had been "added upon," and they were bold in so signifying and exulting.

Someday the boldness of the people of the Church may match the boldness of the doctrines of the Church. Right now, we are rather shy. We don't understand how remarkable as well as plentiful those doctrines are. They contain the answers to the most vexing and searching of all human questions. In fact, through the "restitution of all things," God is actually giving away the secrets of the universe!

However, we need attesting lives as well as tombstones. Attesting lives will be filled with the quiet excitement of constant discovery. There is no boredom in the stretching gospel garden.

Thanks for your desire to do what is right.

Much love,
Grandfather

"It Matters Not"

Dear Michael:

Your friend's illness is a truly poignant situation, especially the way in which he received the sad news about his medical diagnosis. Oh, how frequently waiting for lab reports prolongs the anxiety by their being delayed over a weekend!

Sometimes physical pain represents the scouting column of death. It may go unrecognized by the host simply because so many previous pains proved only transitory, not deadly.

In circumstances such as you describe, the valiant eventually come to realize their pain is different this time. Initial nonrecognition changes to alarm. Reactions, understandably, then usually move on to sorrowing and puzzling wonderment. Finally, however, we watch the valiant become composed, even poised, in their spiritual submission. How we admire and love them all the more!

As we watch them become spiritually settled, they reflect, in their own ways, what Abinadi said of his impending death: "It matters not" (Mosiah 13:9; Mormon 8:4; see also Daniel 3:17). The manner in which they finally and valiantly exit this life actually steadies those of us who remain. We certainly do not envy their ordeal, but we do admire their poise while in passage.

May we be like these Saints when our time comes to notice that first, scouting column of death.

> I love you.
> Grandfather

Brigham Young's Source of Knowledge

Dear Kimball:

Your report on President Brigham Young at our family fireside was excellent! I promised to send you a special insight about why Brigham was so well informed spiritually.

Brigham Young sustained the Prophet Joseph Smith constantly. One special way is interesting: He was always eager to hear Joseph.

> In my experience I never did let an opportunity pass of getting with the Prophet Joseph and of hearing him speak in public or in private, so that I might draw understanding from the fountain from which he spoke, that I might have it and bring it forth when it was needed. . . . In the days of the Prophet Joseph, such moments were more precious to me than all the wealth of the world. No matter how great my poverty—if I had to borrow meal to feed my wife and children, I never let an opportunity pass of learning what the Prophet had to impart.[1]

Brigham listened, Mary-like, to Joseph Smith when Brigham could have been overwhelmed by the Martha-like anxieties of his time. What Brigham heard from Joseph was precious and "was not taken away from him" (see Luke 10:42). What was "not taken" from Brigham has since been shared with all of us.

Brigham Young, by the way, declared of Joseph: "I never called him in question, even in my feelings, for an act of his, except once. I did not like his policy in a matter, and a feeling came into my heart that would have led me to complain; but it was much shorter lived than Jonah's gourd, for it did not last half a minute. Much of Joseph's policy in temporal things was different from my ideas of the way to manage them. He did the best he could, and I do the best I can."[2]

President Young indicated that the isolated occasion of his "want of confidence in Brother Joseph Smith. . . . was not concerning religious matters—it was . . . in relation to his financiering—to his managing the temporal affairs which he undertook." Brigham Young "understood, by the spirit of revelation manifested to me, that if I was to harbour a thought in my heart that Joseph would be wrong in anything, I would begin to lose confidence in him, and that feeling would grow from step to step, and from one degree to another, until at last I would have the same lack of confidence in his being the mouthpiece for the Almighty."[3]

The relationship of Brigham Young to Joseph Smith is fascinating and reassuring for many reasons. Brigham Young's feelings about himself were very modest in relation to his feelings about the Prophet Joseph. When people spoke of his being Joseph's successor, he preferred to characterize himself merely by saying, "I say that I am a good hand to keep the dogs and wolves out of the flock. . . . I do not think anything about being Joseph's successor. That is nothing that concerns me. . . . But, Father, what do you require of me, and what can I do to promote your kingdom on the earth, and save myself and brethren? I do not trouble myself as to whose successor I am."[4]

Yet Brigham Young surely knew who had called him. "I did not desire to be their shepherd; but the great Shepherd of all the sheep placed me in this position, and there is no man on earth can truthfully say aught against the dealings of the leaders of this people with the Latter-day Saints."[5]

Joseph apparently knew from the very beginning of their unique association that Brigham Young would one day preside over the Church.[6] Seeing Brigham's often destitute condition he would caringly, according to Brigham, "often ask me how I lived. I told him I did not know—that I did my best, and the Lord did the rest."[7]

As we are taught by such instructive anecdotes, one of the challenges facing the contemporary Brethren comes to mind: how do we preserve and share the "institutional memory" of the Church, including the more recent instructive anecdotes? Of course, some historical anecdotes are merely humorous, but others are laden with spiritual significance.

The challenge of passing along such informal but instructive things will increase as the Church becomes even more global. Because some local leaders will never be able to leave their flocks and thus rub shoulders with the Brethren and so hear these things directly, other means may need to be devised.

Your report lifted us all the other night, as you who bear one prophet's name described so well another prophet—Brigham!

I love you.
Grandfather

Notes

1. *JD* 12:269–70.
2. *JD* 8:16.
3. *JD* 4:297.
4. *JD* 8:69.
5. *JD* 10:339.
6. See *Millennial Star* 25 (11 July 1863), p. 439.
7. *JD* 7:230.

We Can Have a Fulness of Joy

Dear Ashley:

Your question, "How can we have joy if even just one of our friends is lost?" is a difficult one.

After His resurrection and triumphal atonement Jesus blessed the Nephite children, then saying, "Now behold, my joy is full" (3 Nephi 17:20).

Obviously, Jesus was clearly and fully aware that there were those whose behavior placed them outside the realm of happiness. It is significant, however, that His own happiness was not held hostage thereby. If He who has done so much and who knows perfectly "what might have been" can, nevertheless, rejoice—surely with later and wider perspectives than we now have—we can do likewise.

Furthermore, it will finally be fully demonstrated that all people will receive the *real* desires of their hearts, even if these desires have led to something less than the highest realms of the celestial kingdom (see Jeremiah 17:10; Alma 29:5). All individuals will still openly acknowledge the justice, mercy, and even the unanticipated glory of their situation. To be sure, we will wish much choosing had been otherwise, but in the world to come misery cannot hold joy hostage. Even here and now, the "fruit of the Spirit" is "love, joy, peace" (Galatians 5:22). Moreover, we are, after all, independent beings, as Brigham Young pointed out:

> When God organized intelligent beings, he organized them as independent beings to a certain extent, as he is himself. And whether we see an evil act or a good one performed by an intelligent being, that being has performed the act by his will, by his own independent organization. . . . But we have learned that in our organization we are as independent as the angels are in theirs, or as

any heavenly being that dwells in eternity.[1]

Our happiness as independent beings can finally be maintained independent of the outcomes experienced by others, whether these are exceeding or trailing our own.

Furthermore, when we get our premortal memories back we will see things in a breathtaking scope. There will be precious perspectives which we do not now have. We will, for instance, likely find ourselves rejoicing that we and others have been blessed as much as we have—especially considering God's mercy amid the immutable spiritual laws of the universe upon which all blessings are inevitably and justly based. We will not decline His mercy, nor the proffered degree of glory!

All kingdoms except that which will house the sons of perdition are kingdoms of glory, surpassing all we have known here. Regret will finally be overwhelmed by rejoicing, including our joy over both the justice and the wondrous mercy of God.

Commendations for your own empathy, so highly developed in one so young. I love you.

Grandfather

Notes

1. *JD* 6:146.

The Surprise Visitor

Dear Lauren:

True, when He comes, Jesus will come "as a thief in the night" (1 Thessalonians 5:2). Those unaware will be as if sleeping, only to be interrupted suddenly by the unexpected. The "intruder," however, will be the Lord of the Manor come home!

A secular society is the most likely cultural candidate to be especially surprised by a Jesus who comes "as a thief in the night." A society indifferent, even hostile, to things spiritual will be truly astonished.

The boredom of self-serving secularism and the masking of materialism will cause their devotees to be unaware of events which foretell Christ's coming. One who is wise, however, will take time both to smell the flowers and to check the leaves on the fig tree (see Matthew 24:32).

Equally erroneous expectations are held by those, as prophesied, who will wrongly come to believe that Jesus will come in the form of a woman (see D&C 49:22). The vulnerability to surprise, when the real Jesus comes, will be widely shared.

Jesus foretold that in the last days there would be "distress of nations, with perplexity" (Luke 21:25). "Distress" means great pain, anxiety, sorrow, trouble, or affliction. "Perplexity" means confusion, uncertainty, and bewilderment over situations that are tangled, involved, and complicated. Surely this describes the growing condition of the world. There are so many problems with so many variables and perplexities.

Cut off from traditional, biblical values and from heaven's insights, man—with his lower ways—tries to tackle the world's highest priority problems. No wonder man is perplexed!

Surely, more than ever, the best efforts of good people are needed to solve the challenges of poverty, disease, drugs, pornography, and pollution—whether of the mind or of the air. These problems mount.

When some people cast their eyes upon human history, however, they see only the unbroken sweep of the centuries. Divine interventions seem less and less likely. For these individuals there is no special meaning to human existence. Peter prophesied that some would say, "all things continue as they were from the beginning of the creation" (2 Peter 3:4). So what else is new?

Therefore, in the absence of accepting evidence which is "spiritually discerned"(1 Corinthians 2:14), the passage of time by itself (which actually brings us closer to the resurrection) is ironically seen as a refutation of the resurrection. Misreading small samples is only a variation on the comments of him who confidently concluded, "All Indians walk single file—at least the one I saw did."

I love you.
Grandfather

P.S.

Speaking of being surprised, what, one wonders, were the feelings of the architect for the Tower of Babel? He probably would have been named "architect of the year." But his plans went a floor too far!

Blockages to Spiritual Learning

Dear Timothy:

You will want to ponder this wisdom from Anne Morrow Lindbergh: "I do not believe that sheer suffering teaches. If suffering alone taught, all the world would be wise, since everyone suffers. To suffering must be added mourning, understanding, patience, love, openness, and the willingness to remain vulnerable."[1]

Thus some, like noble and meek Jacob, have their suffering "consecrated" for their personal gain (see 2 Nephi 2:2). Others simply suffer.

Unless suffering is endured well, however, as being related to God's purposes, the gains are anything but automatic. Peter put it well: "If ye be reproached for the name of Christ, happy are ye; for the spirit of glory and of God resteth upon you: on their part he is evil spoken of, but on your part he is glorified. But let none of you suffer as a murderer, or as a thief, or as an evildoer, or as a busybody in other men's matters. Yet if any man suffer as a Christian, let him not be ashamed; but let him glorify God on this behalf." (1 Peter 4:14–16.)

Suffering can be purifying, whereas despair usually drives us to more sin. This is why we are to "school [our] feelings" (*Hymns* no. 6). Tutoring experiences can be for our own good if we let our will be "swallowed up" in the will of God. Then we will learn things we "never had supposed" (Moses 1:10). It's questionable whether or not we can either learn or retain spiritual lessons if we are not meek and humble.

The blockage to learning seems to consist of failure to allow for both the nature of God and the nature of this mortal experience. These two impact continuously upon human nature, and people who don't accept the twin and revealed realities are going to have difficulty in learning.

It should not surprise us, therefore, to learn how anxious God is for us to understand the plan of salvation.

> And they began from that time forth to call on his name; therefore God conversed with men, and made known unto them the plan of redemption, which had been prepared from the foundation of the world; and this he made known unto them according to their faith and repentance and their holy works.
>
> Wherefore, he gave commandments unto men, they having first transgressed the first commandments as to things which were temporal, and becoming as Gods, knowing good from evil, placing themselves in a state to act, or being placed in a state to act according to their wills and pleasures, whether to do evil or to do good—
>
> Therefore God gave unto them commandments, after having made known unto them the plan of redemption, that they should not do evil, the penalty thereof being a second death, which was an everlasting death as to things pertaining unto righteousness; for on such the plan of redemption could have no power, for the works of justice could not be destroyed, according to the supreme goodness of God. (Alma 12:30–32.)

If we don't believe in God, angels, and prophets who receive and transmit revelation, then we will have little faith. We will tend to believe that when a person dies, that is "the end thereof" (Alma 30:18). Revelation is the only way of knowing anything truly significant about God and His purposes, because these things are "spiritually discerned" (1 Corinthians 2:14). As a result, some disbelievers feel that there is no divine law and therefore no real crime, that we fare in this life "according to the management of the creature" (Alma 30:1). This view is "pleasing to the carnal mind," because it seems to release us from any religious restraints. Thus the natural man cuts himself off from light and then complains about the darkness!

The "ways out" of the dilemma are to believe in the reality of the rescuing Christ. But some believe there shall be "no

Christ," and that we "cannot know there shall be a Christ" (Alma 30:12). Further, we "cannot know" about anything we "do not see" (Alma 30:15). So, such conclude, a rescuing Christ is not a possibility.

Vital to accessing a "way out" is the perspective which comes from prophecy. But if some are disposed to believe that "no man can know of anything which is to come," prophecy's "way out" is also blocked. (See Alma 30:13–15.)

If we can have a belief in the reality of personal immortality, including personal accountability, this is part of the "way out." But when some believe "that when a man [is] dead, that [is] the end thereof" (Alma 30:18), that "way out" is also blocked.

Believing in the moral absolutes is a requisite to the "way out." However, if some are disposed to believe "that whatsoever a man did was no crime" (Alma 30:17), then that "way out" is likewise blocked. Thus we remain entrapped! How much of the human predicament consists of these blockages?

Eternal love,
Grandfather

P.S.

By the way, I have always had a special appreciation for my friends who, though resolutely irreligious themselves, were not scoffers. Instead, though doubtless puzzled by me and their other religious friends, they were nevertheless respectful. I admire the day-to-day decency seen in such men and women. Though detached from theology, their decency is so commendable.

Notes

1. Brigham Young University *Law Review*, 1991, no. 1.

Mortal Joys Foreshadow Immortality

Dear Katie:

Yes, the beautiful and variously colored flowers of spring and summer wither so quickly. Likewise, the gorgeous, configuring clouds pass so soon. The breathtaking sunsets last for mere moments before fading into gray darkness. We wish we could somehow cling to these.

Such is this life's relentless passing of things. We cannot help but notice, can we? There are so many pointed reminders of our passing mortality, each sharpened by the extensive and luxuriant beauty in this world.

By the way, how many people do you know whose favorite color is gray? Our Lord's creations are many splendored; He loves beauty and color!

These passing joys enrich us now, but they serve yet another purpose by providing a mild foretaste of unceasing immortality.

Fortunately, while "the grass withereth, [and] the flower fadeth . . . the word of our God shall stand for ever" (Isaiah 40:8).

But life is not all beauty and ease. Brigham Young counseled: "Facts are made apparent to the human mind by their opposites. We find ourselves surrounded in this mortality by an almost endless combination of opposites, through which we must pass to gain experience and information to fit us for an eternal progression."[1] Experience can impress upon us the needed learning, making it more deep and lasting. Pain can make impressions on the tablets of memory. Minus the relevant personal experience, however, neither logic nor abstraction could teach us so directly, deeply, lastingly, and personally as can experience.

If we are meek, even frustrations can teach us. George MacDonald wrote that many of the difficulties of discipleship occur simply because of the rigors experienced when "the pilgrim must be headed back from the side paths into which he is constantly wandering."[2] Retracing can be time-consuming and frustrating; repetition of the deviation, however, is thereby discouraged.

Individualized experience thus has its own exclusive way of teaching. We do not, however, automatically learn from experience any more than we do by merely being present in school.

Could we, later on, appreciate the endlessness of immortality without poignant reminders of our passing mortality? Could we be ready for the brightness of the perfect day without previously experiencing some darkness? Could we be as well prepared for rich reunions without present deprivations and separations? More than we know, so many present things are given to us precisely in order to increase our capacity for eternal appreciation.

We thus come to discover, by our own experience, the differences not only between pain and pleasure but also between mere pleasure and real joy. Meanwhile, however, the curtains poignantly close on various mortal scenes, scenes which we would prolong if only we could. These present cessations are real—sometimes painfully real—but they are only an interruption preceding immortality. Today's moments are mere dots on the canvas of eternity.

Your consistent concern for doing what is right, combined with your effervescence, is impressive. Anyone who has such enduring enthusiasm for this life will be ever joyful amid eternity.

I love you.
Grandfather

Notes

1. *JD* 11:42.
2. Quoted in *Around the Year*, October 16.

Prayers Are Petitions

Dear Peter:

We have a duty to pray always (see Luke 18:1; 21:36; 1 Thessalonians 5:17). We have been taught the manner of prayer, both explicitly and implicitly (see Luke 11:1–13).

Further, we are told that, given God's omniscience, He knows beforehand what we will ask for (see Matthew 6:8). Hence our prayers are not the means of briefing God. Prayer is a petition from us, not information for Him (see Philippians 4:6). We are invited, however, to petition Him honestly, frequently, and straightforwardly, including in the request our flocks and other personal concerns (see Alma 34:17–27).

Yet prayers, which come so naturally to the child, are difficult for the "natural man." The process can be puzzling at times even for some sincere petitioners. Paul gave us this personal insight on the importance of our being guided by the Spirit as we pray: "Likewise the Spirit also helpeth our infirmities: *for we know not what we should pray for as we ought*: but the Spirit itself maketh intercession for us with groanings which cannot be uttered" (Romans 8:26, emphasis added).

Some have difficulty with the reality that prayers are petitions even though God knows all and loves all anyway. True, we are not informing God, but we are informing ourselves by reverently working through our real concerns and our real priorities and by listening to the Spirit. For us merely to say, ritualistically, "Thy will be done" would not be real petitionary prayer. This would involve no genuine working through of our own feelings. There would be no experience in agonizing, in choosing, and also in submitting.

Jesus' ultimate prayer in Gethsemane, "Take this cup from me" was not theater, it was real pleading! But it was followed by real submitting! (See Mark 14:35–36.) When Jesus entered Gethsemane He "fell on the ground" (Mark 14:35).

He "fell on his face, and prayed" (Matthew 26:39). "Being in an agony, he prayed more earnestly" (Luke 22:44).

Furthermore, since we are told by God that we receive no blessings except by obedience to the laws upon which those blessings are predicated (see D&C 130:20–21), prayer is required as part of that process of learning to ask for what is right. "And this is the confidence that we have in him, that, if we ask any thing according to his will, he heareth us" (1 John 5:14; see also 3 Nephi 18:20; James 4:3; 2 Nephi 4:35).

We cannot expect the blessings of prayer unless we submit sincerely, meekly, and fully to the process of prayer.

Granted, finite minds do not fully understand the infinite mind of God. We are not fully comprehending when our agency brushes against His divinity. Yet we should trust Him as our provincial petitions meet His universal omniscience.

King Lamoni's father, for instance, uncertain whether there actually was a God, used these words: "If there is a God." His was a genuine pleading followed by a genuine offering to "give away all my sins to know thee." (Alma 22:18.)

It is necessary for us thus to place our desires and needs genuinely and unselfishly before God in prayer. It is in this process of placing our desires before Him, to a greater extent than we usually do, that we can listen and learn concerning His will. Such could not be done if we were ritualistically submissive or only partially involved.

Of course, after we place our petitions before Him we are to be submissive: "Thy will be done." But this is the last part of the process of petition, not the first.

Learning to pray is, therefore, the work of a lifetime. If we keep on praying, we will keep on discovering.

Much love,
Grandpa

This Truth Is Spiritually Discerned

Dear Brittany:

When some scoff at the reality of underlying spiritual purposes for the human family, they are scoffing at perspectives which are "spiritually discerned" (1 Corinthians 2:14). Such people resemble Galileo's provincial friends who spurned the invitation to look through his mind-expanding telescope for fear of what they would see!

In the last days the predicted scoffers say, "Where is the promise of his coming?" (2 Peter 3:4.) They ignore the signaling leaves on the fig tree (see Matthew 24:32). Nevertheless, one day "all flesh," including the presently unnoticing and distracted, "shall see [Him] together" (D&C 101:23).

Without a view of truth which is spiritually discerned it is so easy to "charge God foolishly," when instead we should worship Him reverently (Job 1:22).

As to the scoffing of your acquaintance, from what you have reported there seems to be no need to worry. Sometimes those we meet are merely sheep in wolves' clothing. Not only real wolves travel in packs; so, sometimes, do sheep disguised as wolves. They do not blush over their pack mentality. The Gadarene group thundered on their destructive way to the sea (see Luke 8:26–33), probably imagining all the while that they were actually rugged individualists!

I love you.
Grandfather

The Word of God

Dear Brian:

You're right; some employ the phrase "word of the Lord" carelessly at times. Paul declared, "The sword of the Spirit . . . is the word of God" (Ephesians 6:17).

When "the word" is described by Paul as "quick," this denotes, in the Greek, "living." It is significant that The Church of Jesus Christ of Latter-day Saints has been described as "the only true and living church" (D&C 1:30)—with living prophets. Unsurprisingly, it also has a living and ever-expanding canon of scripture. Much more scripture is to come. (See 2 Nephi 29:13, 14; D&C 107:56–57; Articles of Faith 1:9.)

We likewise read that God's word is "piercing." His precision is joined with His power: "For the word of God is quick, and powerful, and sharper than any two-edged sword, piercing even to the dividing asunder of soul and spirit, and of the joints and marrow, and is a discerner of the thoughts and intents of the heart" (Hebrews 4:12; see also D&C 33:1).

No wonder it is so, for "these words are not of men nor of man, but of me; wherefore, you shall testify they are of me and not of man" (D&C 18:34). Nephi said meekly and accurately of his writings, "Believe in these words, for they are the words of Christ, and he hath given them unto me" (2 Nephi 33:10). Little wonder, given such circumstances, that "the word had . . . more powerful effect upon the minds of the people than . . . anything else" (Alma 31:5).

Certain gospel words, concepts, or phrases seem to have been singularly sanctified by God. Especially designed to elicit particular responses, they seem to carry a distinctive, evocative power. Though used in different dispensations and uttered by different prophets, such concepts appear to persist in a steady, spiritual state.

For all we now know, the special, evocative powers of

certain words and doctrines are linked with flashes of our memory from the premortal world. At least, they connect up with any righteous predispositions nurtured there. Moreover, whether written or spoken, when they are impelled by the Spirit it is the same.

We all know of Joseph Smith's special experience in reading James's words written centuries earlier: "Never did any passage of scripture come with more power to the heart of man than this did at this time to mine. It seemed to enter with great force into every feeling of my heart." (Joseph Smith—History 1:12.)

Doubtless James's words had helped many prior to that spring day in 1820, but those words were also meant to be especially evocative, for so much was impending, as Joseph was to become this dispensation's most remarkable conduit: "This generation shall have my word through you" (D&C 5:10).

So often it starts with beginners meekly trusting in the inspired words of the already faithful: "Faith in the words alone of my servant" (Mosiah 26:15). "And now if thou sayest there is a God, behold I will believe" (Alma 22:7). Such discipleship brings its own rewards: "Blessed are they because of their exceeding faith in the words alone which thou hast spoken unto them" (Mosiah 26:16).

The steadying word of God has also been defined as "the iron rod" (1 Nephi 11:25). At His second coming the Lord will rule with that rod of iron—not a metallic scepter, of course—and those words will form His laws and directions (see Revelation 19:15).

"The word," if "sufficiently retained in remembrance" (Alma 5:6), is powerful in its capacity to evoke precious memories:

> And it came to pass that as I was thus racked with torment, while I was harrowed up by the memory of my many sins, behold, I remembered also to have heard my father prophesy unto the people concerning the coming of one Jesus Christ, a Son of God, to atone for the sins of the world.

Now, as my mind caught hold upon this thought, I cried within my heart: O Jesus, thou Son of God, have mercy on me, who am in the gall of bitterness, and am encircled about by the everlasting chains of death. (Alma 36:17–18.)

The word can also "prick" hearts and stir us up "to repentance" (Jarom 1:12). How vital such divine discontent can be, especially for "hearts set so much upon the things of this world" (D&C 121:35). Such hearts must often be pierced, even broken, before a new heart can function.

Contemplation of the existing scriptures has often fortuitously led to the revelation of additional scriptures. The splendid revelations known now as sections 138 and 76 of the Doctrine and Covenants came to us in this very manner: "On the third of October, in the year nineteen hundred and eighteen, I sat in my room pondering over the scriptures" (D&C 138:1). "Accordingly, while translating St. John's Gospel, myself and Elder Rigdon saw the following vision" (D&C 76 headnote).

The spiritual electricity thus arcs from one cluster of special concepts and words to bring forth another such cluster!

However, in partaking of the word of God for maximum personal value, it is imperative that we do as Nephi did: "And I did read many things unto them which were written in the books of Moses; but that I might more fully persuade them to believe in the Lord their Redeemer I did read unto them that which was written by the prophet Isaiah; for I did *liken all scriptures unto us*, that it might be *for our profit and learning* (1 Nephi 19:23, emphasis added).

Pondering both during and after reading the word helps us to so "liken."

Pondering, for most of us, is not something we do easily. It is much more than drifting or daydreaming, for it focuses and stirs us, not lulls us. We must set aside time, circumstances, and attitude in order to achieve it. In Alma's words, we must "give place" (Alma 32:27). The length of time involved in pondering is not as important as the intensity given to it. Reflection cannot be achieved in the midst of distraction.

Cumulatively, the word of God reflects the rich, historical goodness of God to man. This is described in a neglected verse which precedes one that receives much attention: "Behold, I would exhort you that when ye shall read these things . . . that ye would remember how merciful the Lord hath been unto the children of men, from the creation of Adam even down unto the time that ye shall receive these things, and ponder it in your hearts" (Moroni 10:3).

By preserving the past, God gives us guidance for the future. This is the "navigational" role of holy scripture, likewise vital, for each of us. "Yea, we see that whosoever will may lay hold upon the word of God, which is quick and powerful, which shall divide asunder all the cunning and the snares and the wiles of the devil, and lead the man of Christ in a strait and narrow course across that everlasting gulf of misery which is prepared to engulf the wicked" (Helaman 3:29).

Since the gaping "gulf of misery" is very real, no wonder we must be invigorated by "feasting upon the word of Christ" (2 Nephi 31:20) if we expect to stay the course and stay on course.

The scriptures perform yet another vital task. They enlarge the memory by incorporating the collective, spiritual memory of past ages into one's own (see Alma 37:8). The scriptures thus permit us to access decades of divine data, the "institutional memory" of God's people. "For whatsoever things were written aforetime were written for our learning, that we through patience and comfort of the scriptures might have hope" (Romans 15:4).

Samuel Johnson observed "people more frequently need to be reminded than instructed."[1] If heeded, the lessons from the past can deflect us from present wrong ways or wrong intents. "All scripture is given by inspiration of God, and is profitable for doctrine, for reproof, for correction, for instruction in righteousness" (2 Timothy 3:16).

Sometimes people are willing to hear "a voice from the dust" when they will not listen to a contemporary voice of a loving parent, spouse, or child. The sweep of scriptural history makes accessible the cumulative and "sad experience" of yesterday's sinners.

Various verses contain sting one-liners for unfaithful "two-timers." They provide instructive case studies for egoists who have "a case" on themselves! Similarly, the scriptures contain sobering words for those who are intoxicated by riches, power, or the praise of men.

Of course, most people remain unreached by the scriptures. Their scriptures go unread, unheeded, or unpondered. Still others skim the scriptures mechanically, remaining untouched by their beauty and relevancy.

Though reading the word of the Lord, some of us are slow to see the obvious connection between related verses. For instance, do most of us quickly make a connection between the words of King Benjamin (saying that each of us should be "willing to submit to all things which the Lord seeth fit to inflict upon him, even as a child doth submit to his father") and words in Mark ("Abba, Father, all things are possible unto thee; take away this cup from me: nevertheless not what I will, but what thou wilt")? (Mosiah 3:19; Mark 14:36.)

Do we see the connection, too, between such words as, "They did suffer much, both *in body* and *in mind*, such as hunger, thirst and fatigue, and also much labor in the spirit" and Jesus' words about the Atonement, "which suffering caused myself, even God, the greatest of all, to tremble because of pain, and to bleed at every pore, and to suffer *both body and spirit* . . ." (Alma 17:5; D&C 19:18, emphasis added)? Or between that statement and these words: "Yea, and they were *depressed in body as well as in Spirit* . . . they had suffered great afflictions of every kind" (Alma 56:16, emphasis added)?

Each of these scriptures suggests the interactiveness of pain involving body and mind or body and spirit. Jesus' was the ultimate and most excruciating form of interactive pain. Mark (14:33) describes Jesus in Gethsemane as being "very heavy," meaning, in the Greek, depressed.

The scriptures can give us needed rock-like steadiness, especially in this latter-day, topsy-turvy world in which "all things are in commotion" (D&C 45:26; 88:91).

Consciences, sharpened by the scriptures, can be like

pointers that work according to our faith (see 1 Nephi 16:28). Furthermore, who among us has not had the experience of opening the scriptures randomly only to focus on a much needed verse?

The scriptures—searched and applied—also can ensure that we will think more upon Jesus, instead of moving, lamentably, in the opposite direction in our embracing of the cares of the world. "For how knoweth a man the master whom he has not served, and who is a stranger unto him, and is far from the thoughts and intents of his heart?" (Mosiah 5:13.)

No wonder we are encouraged to first "try the virtue of the word of God" (Alma 31:5). Otherwise, Jesus will become far from our thoughts, and we will be estranged from our best friend.

Thanks for being patient in reading this "heavy" letter, but your query was not a light one.

> With love and admiration,
> Grandfather

P.S.

Elsewhere, I have written of "imperial scriptures," meaning those scriptures that touch us deeply and extend themselves over so many circumstances. Each of us ought to have a few of these, and they should be memorized and pondered from time to time as if they were an evaluative screen we can spread over our circumstances. A few key imperial scriptures can humble us throughout our entire lives—if we will but remember them.

Notes

1. Quoted in *Around the Year*, August 2.

One True Church,
but Much Goodness Elsewhere Too

Dear Lindsey:

You wonder about how the Restoration's exclusivity comes across to others. One important thing we can do, as Church members, is to gladly and spontaneously rejoice over how much good so many other people do and in so many good causes! Jesus so responded to offset the wonderment of His meridian disciples who were concerned over good deeds being done by some who apparently were not of Jesus' flock: "And John answered him, saying, Master, we saw one casting out devils in thy name, and he followeth not us: and we forbad him, because he followeth not us. But Jesus said, Forbid him not: for there is no man which shall do a miracle in my name, that can lightly speak evil of me. For he that is not against us is on our part. For whosoever shall give you a cup of water to drink in my name, because ye belong to Christ, verily I say unto you, he shall not lose his reward." (Mark 9:38–41.)

Our zeal must never lead to intolerance. Nor should we restrain our rejoicing in all good deeds.

In fact, Mormon revealed that "all things which are good cometh of God" (Moroni 7:12). Therefore, we should sincerely rejoice in all goodness.

By the way, you have always applauded the accomplishments of your own brothers and sisters—even when the family focus, for the moment, was on some of them, leaving you less noticed. Yet you were genuinely glad and still achieved significantly anyway.

I love you.
Grandfather

Giving and Receiving Reproof

Dear Ryan:

You are right. Joseph Smith's rebuke of the guards at the Richmond, Missouri, jail is a classic!

Reproof can come in many forms. The wise learn from experience when there are those who are willing to tutor. William Pitt, one of England's first prime ministers, came on too strong in Parliament as a young man in attacking Horace Walpole. He was reproved by others and also in his own mind.[1] He was wise enough to learn from that episode in his "sophomore days." Later he became an esteemed figure, able even to challenge George III over the rights of the American colonies. Pitt learned to bide his time, however, and not to overdo his oratory.

Young Winston Churchill was too sarcastic and too prepared on one occasion when he was first in Parliament. One of the senior members of Parliament, Balfour, reproved him in these words:

> As for the junior member for Oldham, his speech was certainly not remarkable for good taste, and as I have always taken an interest in that honorable Gentleman's career, I should certainly, if I thought it in the least good, offer him some advice on that particular subject. But I take it that good taste is not a thing that can be acquired by industry, and that even advice of a most heartfelt and genuine description would entirely fail in effect if I were to offer it to him. But on another point I think I may give him some advice which may be useful to him in the course of what I hope will be a long and distinguished career. It is not, on the whole, desirable to come down to this House with invective which is both prepared and vio-

lent. The House will tolerate, and very rightly tolerate, almost anything within the rule of order which evidently springs from genuine indignation aroused by the collision of debate. But to come down with these prepared phrases is not usually successful, and at all events, I do not think it was very successful on the present occasion. If there is preparation there should be more finish, and if there is so much violence there should certainly be more veracity of feeling.[2]

General George Washington reproved rebellious officers who were involved in what was called the Newburgh Plot. He did it with a most gentle form of reproof, the authority of example:

> Washington called together the grumbling officers on March 15, 1783. . . . He began to speak—carefully and from a written manuscript. . . . Washington appealed simply and honestly for reason, restraint, patience, and duty—all the good and unexciting virtues.
>
> And then Washington stumbled as he read. He squinted, paused, and out of his pocket he drew some new spectacles. "Gentlemen, you must pardon me," he said in apology. "I have grown gray in your service and now find myself growing blind."
>
> Most of his men had never seen the general wear glasses. Yes, the men said to themselves, eight hard years. They recalled the ruddy, full-blooded planter of 1775; now they saw . . . a big, good, fatherly man grown old. They wept, many of those warriors. And the Newburgh Plot dissolved.[3]

Surely in Washington's case Plato's dictum was observed: "Access to power must be confined to men who are not in love with it."[4] Revelation tells us "that the powers of heaven cannot be controlled nor handled only upon the principles of righteousness" (D&C 21:36).

The skillful and loving giving of reproof is as vital as is the meek receiving of it. Both components need to be present for the learning to be fully effective, and we are all spiritual neighbors.

Much love,
Grandfather

Notes

1. See J. C. Long, *Mr. Pitt* (New York: Frederick A. Stokes Co., 1940), p. 93.

2. Quoted in Ted Morgan, *Churchill, Young Man in a Hurry, 1874–1915* (New York: Simon and Schuster, 1982), p. 175.

3. Bart McDowell, *The Revolutionary War* (Washington, D.C.: National Geographic Society, 1967), pp. 190–91.

4. Quoted in Richard Hazelett and Dean Turner, *Benevolent Living* (Pasadena: Hope Publishing, 1990), p. 181.

Dealing with Doubters

Dear Martha:

You are quite right to be lovingly concerned about doubters, who come in such various shapes and attitudinal shadings. Some doubters truly seek answers. These give the Brethren the benefit of the doubt, and, for them, doubt becomes a useful spiritual spur.

There are others who doubt and hold back simply because they are so afraid of being "taken in."

There are still others who are embarrassed because of their inability to defend their faith; for these, doubt is a refuge. Yet other doubters are stubborn, because they feel God has not responded to them on their terms. There are even doubters who come to enjoy their roles and the associated attention and who set themselves up "as a golden calf for the worship" of people in the Church (D&C 124:84). A variation of the latter is seen in those who are "professing and yet [are] not of God" (D&C 46:27; see also D&C 136:19). "He commandeth that there shall be no priestcrafts; for, behold, priestcrafts are that men preach and set themselves up for a light unto the world, that they may get gain and praise of the world; but they seek not the welfare of Zion" (2 Nephi 26:29).

These latter individuals have their own agendum and have apparently long since concluded that, if they can't be a leader, then they will be a critic.

Doubters often pool their doubts by associating with like-minded individuals, each bringing his own favorite "dish" as if to a potluck dinner.

If the doubter is one of our loved ones we can learn, first-hand, how to balance our concern for the welfare of such with the need for him or her to exercise moral agency. Our mercy meets his agency. Clearly, our efforts to teach should blend exhortation, explanation, and example. Understandably, a father or a mother so situated becomes, like Lehi, "a trembling parent" (2 Nephi 1:14).

Absent sufficient meekness in the doubter, I am not sure that much can be done. Experience can either soften or harden doubts, depending on the person's supply of meekness. Clearly, however, our love should include all doubters, whatever their motivation, "for ye know not but what they will . . . come unto me with full purpose of heart" (3 Nephi 18:32).

I love you and your ever-contagious smile.

Grandfather

Shaped by Experience

Dear Sarah Jane:

As we ponder the importance of learning by our own experience, we sense all the more that in our first estate we were told things now forgotten and we saw things with a wider perspective. We, at that point, had not had the personally validating experiences. Without these our determination to support divine standards would have lacked the full weight of personal verification. Thus Brigham Young explained: "It has also been decreed by the Almighty that spirits, upon taking bodies, shall forget all they had known previously, or they could not have a day of trial—could not have an opportunity for proving themselves in darkness and temptation, in unbelief and wickedness, to prove themselves worthy of eternal existence.[1]

Mortality now supplies experiences that are to be joined one day with those experiences of the first estate—to trust God for whatever lies ahead. The validation, by our own experience, of God's plans, principles, and doctrines in two estates will not only increase our appreciation of Him but will also bring about our adoration of Him. We can then teach with authenticity as well as authority.

There is a real difference between knowing personally and "knowing" but only as a result of logical extrapolations. In the first estate we had been taught about as much as we could be taught about some things by *explanation*. The time had come for us to learn by validating personal *experiences*. So for now, we walk by faith.

Two separate episodes illustrate the importance of initial faith followed by personal validation.

Behold, I say unto you they are made known unto me by the Holy Spirit of God. Behold, I have fasted and prayed many days that I might know these things of myself. And now I do know of myself that they are true; for the Lord God hath made them manifest unto me by his Holy Spirit; and this is the spirit of revelation which is in me. (Alma 5:46.)

And many of the Samaritans of that city believed on him for the saying of the woman, which testified, He told me all that ever I did.

So when the Samaritans were come unto him, they besought him that he would tarry with them: and he abode there two days.

And many more believed because of his own word;

And said unto the woman, Now we believe, not because of thy saying: for we have heard him ourselves, and know that this is indeed the Christ, the Saviour of the world. (John 4:39–42; see also D&C 46:13–14.)

Jesus spoke of doing and thereby knowing about God's doctrines: "If any man will do his will, he shall know of the doctrine, whether it be of God, or whether I speak of myself" (John 7:17). Alma said the same thing: Even if we have no more than a desire to believe, by giving place and nurturing the gospel seed we can cause desire to soon grow unto belief, which, in turn, will grow unto faith, which can then grow unto knowledge "in that thing" (Alma 32:34). Brigham Young concurred with Alma, stating that each principle of the gospel carries with it its own witness that it is true, that "every principle God has revealed carries its own convictions of its truth to the human mind"[2]

Yes, we learn precept by precept, but also experience by experience. Subsequent experiences confirm and reconfirm what we already know intellectually. The learning needs to be deep enough, however, to survive the erosion which can occur with the passage of time. As with Moses, new experiences help us to explore truths and realities which we "never had supposed" (Moses 1:10).

Why, then, are some things so hard?

Though the record in Brigham Young's office journal of

1857 is not complete, he apparently was asked, "Why are [we] left alone and often sad?" His response was that man has to learn to "act as an independent being . . . to see what he will do . . . to practice him . . . to be righteous in the dark—to be the friend of God."[3]

Of the sometimes muddled middle, Elder Erastus Snow commented: "The Lord has shown us both ends of the drama. As to the particular scenery of the different parts of the drama, it will be made manifest from time to time." Elder Snow advises us that God is a "good manager, and . . . is moving upon the checker-board of nations, and he understands the game and will make the right moves." Besides, continued Elder Snow, "if all the details were made known unto us—if we could see every minutia portrayed, would there be a chance for the exercise of our faith in the same degree as now?"

Will we be perplexed? Indeed, we are at times, because "often the Lord shapes trials in a manner different from our expectations. We, in our limited capacity, may mark out, in our minds a programme; and when he moves upon the checker-board, he does not move the men we have in our minds, but he shapes and moves in another way; and we should be satisfied with the result."[4]

We cannot control the coming of life's crises, but we can control how we respond to them.

Sometimes things are made hard so as to be hard to forget. At other times we ourselves make things unnecessarily hard simply because we are torn between competing desires and loyalties.

The needed insights can come with the ministrations of the Lord's Spirit. "For behold, again I say unto you . . . the Holy Ghost, . . . will show unto you all things what ye should do" (2 Nephi 32:5).

The Spirit is a resolver because it also is a clarifier. It shows us the truth of "things as they really are" (Jacob 4:13).

Still, much of life's opposition is of our own making. We would be embarrassed to see how much of our own difficulty really comes from ourselves. Things are harder precisely because we ourselves make them harder, because of our procrastination, our ambivalence, or our lack of obedience and courage. Any needless deviations or wanderings, for instance, require the painful, time-consuming retracing of our steps, costing both energy and time. It is especially embarrassing, fatiguing, and frustrating to undo the gnarled knot of our own mistakes.

The natural man is, therefore, truly an enemy to God, because he is an enemy to God's children. He validates Pogo's "We have met the enemy and he is us!" And he is the most frequent obstructionist to happiness.

Take, for instance, how we attempt to set aside, or at least bend, a principle in order to be "well liked." It seems so incidental at the time, but we mistakenly soften our integrity in order to manifest empathy. Or we may simply "let down" for a brief moment, allowing ourselves to be carried willingly along on some froth of circumstance, even while knowing we must soon trudge back after the easy exhilaration of the moment is over!

I love you for blending meekness and brightness.

Grandfather

P.S.

Even if we don't like it, we should recognize divine tutoring when it comes, which is needed to overcome our drift. It is part of being intellectually honest. Eli, who had served the Lord well, was reproved by the Lord for his failures as a too indulgent father. Nevertheless, when the message came Eli said, "It is the Lord" (1 Samuel 3:18). Painful as the message was, he did not resent the young messenger. Perhaps the reproof was not unexpected.

Would that we were all so able to receive a needed message without resenting the messenger!

Notes

1. *JD* 7:193.
2. *JD* 9:149.
3. Brigham Young's office journal, Wednesday, 28 January 1857.
4. *JD* 5:301.

Why Don't We Understand?

Dear Robbie:

Several times the Lord has asked His followers why they could not understand certain things. He knew why, of course, but He inquired instructively. (See D&C 50:21, 31; 9:7; 78:17.) In these cases, the failure was an inability to see the obvious because of one variation or another of "looking beyond the mark" (Jacob 4:14).

Why don't we ponder the obvious more? Sometimes we refuse to explore the truth of a doctrine simply because we think we already grasp it fully; we imagine we are "past" it. Sometimes, however, it is because we do not really wish to face a doctrine's implications. Consider such central doctrines as the foreknowledge of God, the moral agency of man, how blessings are tied to our obedience to God's laws, or the whole array of scriptures which advise us that this life is to be a proving experience. All of these contain profound implications for each of us in our daily lives as well as in eternity. But how often do we really deal with these along with their implications instead of turning away from them?

Laman and Lemuel, for example, were aware of God's dramatic rescue of ancient Israel from mighty Pharaoh and his thousands, but they could not see its clear implications for calming their fear of Laban—a local power figure—with his mere fifty! (See 1 Nephi 4:1.)

Another example: Only by persisting in His questioning did Jesus succeed in getting His disciples to remember that there were actually twelve baskets of "leftovers" *after* the miracle of the loaves (see Matthew 14:15–21; 16:9–10). The Bread of Life always gives "enough and to spare" (D&C 104:17), but we're so forgetful.

When we understand the obvious more fully, many other things will become more clear to us as well.

I love you. Continue to search and ponder the scriptures, as you've done from childhood.

Grandfather

"Mystic Chords of Memory"

Dear Lindsey:

You are quite right; memories do seem to be enhanced and enriched with the passage of time. It is not something to worry about especially, however.

You may recall that Abraham Lincoln spoke in his First Inaugural Address, though with a different emphasis, about "mystic chords of memory." Just how and why those chords vibrate and interplay, collectively and individually, remains for now a mystic thing.

In support of your observation, here is a brief C. S. Lewis quote from an unpublished poem of his friend, Owen Barfield. Barfield noted that our experiences may be "a whisper, which Memory will warehouse as a shout.¹

Probably the restless mind, blocked as it is from premortal memories, does tend to enhance. Some inflation, however, is only to be a preparation for what lies ahead which "eye hath not seen, nor ear heard" (1 Corinthians 2:9).

Even the gospel glimpses are difficult to convey. Brigham Young said, "I cannot talk all my feelings, I cannot tell you what I feel and what I see in the Spirit."² This inability to articulate concerns not only the grand and sacred things but also the simple joys of faith: "I cannot say the smallest part which I feel" (Alma 26:16). Thus it is not only that our eyes and ears have not yet experienced what lies ahead; even if they had, the tongue could not fully express our feelings in the face of such sublime and reassuring things! President Brigham Young's words remind us of Jacob's: "If I could take away the vail, and let you see how *things really are*, you would then know just as well as I know, and I know them just as well as any man on the face of the earth need to."³

The Spirit enhances perspective. Elder John Taylor observed: "When the light of heaven comes to reflect upon the human mind, when we can see ourselves as God sees us and comprehend ourselves as he comprehends us . . . we should have different views of ourselves than we have when unenlightened by the Spirit."[4]

Given the role of memory, there is reason for us to so live as to make needed memories deliberately, memories which can nourish us in the years ahead.

One day we will have total recall. What a marvelous moment lies ahead, when the memories of the premortal world merge with those of the mortal world to prepare us to live in "one eternal 'now' "![5]

Your loving Grandfather

Notes

1. Wayne Martindale and Jerry Roob, eds., *The Quotable C. S. Lewis* (Wheaton, Illinois: Tyndale Publications, 1989), p. 424.

2. *JD* 4:373.

3. *JD* 3:223, emphasis added. See also Jacob 4:13.

4. *JD* 10:147.

5. *Teachings*, p. 220.

Jesus Christ Our Lord

Dear Grandchildren:

Some years ago, during a Christmas season I gave a talk entitled, "Jesus, Lord of the Universe and Lord of Loving-Kindness." I am sending it along at least for your files, if not for your hearts. You will recognize a few things from other letters sent to you.

Jesus, Lord of the Universe and Lord of Loving-Kindness

I come in this season as a special witness of Jesus Christ to tell you of my love for Him and, more important, His perfect love for all of us! Of all things for which we should be thankful, nothing exceeds the gift of Jesus' atonement.

We refer to Him variously and simply as the Man of Galilee, Jesus of Nazareth, the Christ Child, the Babe born at Bethlehem, or the Master. The inherent meekness of His mortal messiahship allows for such reverent expressions. In fact, during His ministry as the Mortal Messiah He was known by some merely as "the carpenter's son" (see Philippians 2:7; Matthew 13:55).

Yet even though His marvelous meekness permits Him to be so designated, we should ever remember and consider who He really is, especially when we ponder and consider Him in His majesty. He is actually the Lord of a far-flung vineyard, Lord of the universe. After the mind-expanding parable contained in section 88 of the Doctrine and Covenants we read, "I leave these sayings with you to ponder in your hearts" (D&C 88:62).

God the Father is the God of "the earth and all the planets." He comprehends them all (see D&C 88:43, 61). Under His direction, Jesus, the "carpenter's son," helped to build an undisclosed portion of the universe! "That by [Jesus], and through him, and of him, the worlds are and were created, and the inhabitants thereof are begotten sons and daughters unto God" (D&C 76:24).

How many worlds, we do not know. Which are inhabited we do not know. Earth appears to be the only inhabited world in our own solar system. However, when gazing heavenward and contemplating even the least of all the planets, we see God "moving in his majesty and power" (D&C 88:47).

Even so, as with Moses, "only an account of this earth, and the inhabitants thereof" (Moses 1:35) has been given us.

Most people living on this planet He created do not really know who Christ is or what He has done for us or what He will yet do. Too many think of Him, if they think of Him at all, merely as an outstanding moral teacher or perhaps a minor prophet. But to our joy the hundreds of pages of additional Restoration scriptures testify of His divinity and messiahship and amplify our knowledge of Him. After all, it was He who announced that the "scriptures . . . testify of me" (John 5:39).

Ponder these words concerning the central purposes of the Restoration: "And righteousness will I send down out of heaven; and truth will I send forth out of the earth." Messengers from heaven and the coming forth of the Book of Mormon—to do what? "To bear testimony of mine Only Begotten; his resurrection from the dead; yea, and also the resurrection of all men." (Moses 7:62.)

Are any truths and reassurances more desperately needed today by billions of mortals?

The more we know of Jesus, the more we come to love Him! As our adoration of Jesus deepens, it produces genuine emulation of Him. We desire to be with Him and to be more like Him. The Prophet Joseph instructed, "If you wish to go where God is, you must be like God . . . [in] the principles which God possesses."[1]

Our trials and troubles, much as we would avoid them, are the relevant developmental experiences, if we will accept them as such. The perspective of the gospel is so vital. Hear Brigham Young:

We talk about our trials and troubles here in this life:
but suppose that you could see yourselves thousands and
millions of years after you have proved faithful to your religion during the few short years in this time, and have
obtained eternal salvation and a crown of glory in the
presence of God; then look back upon your lives here,
and see the losses, crosses, and disappointments, the sor-
rows . . . you would be constrained to exclaim, "But what
of all that? Those things were but for a moment, and we
are now here. We have been faithful during a few moments in our mortality, and now we enjoy eternal life and
glory, with power to progress in all the boundless knowledge and through the countless stages of progression, en-
joying the smiles and approbation of our Father and God,
and of Jesus Christ our elder brother."[2]

Illustrative examples follow concerning Jesus' dealings
with His sheep. Some show how personal He is. Some illustrate how global, even universal, He is.

First, to those at Jerusalem the Mortal Messiah declared:
"And other sheep I have, which are not of this fold: them also
I must bring, and they shall hear my voice; and there shall be
one fold, and one shepherd" (John 10:16).

His provincial audience did not understand. Later, to
those in the Americas, the resurrected Jesus declared: "And
verily I say unto you, that ye are they of whom I said: Other
sheep I have which are not of this fold; them also I must
bring, and they shall hear my voice; and there shall be one
fold, and one shepherd" (3 Nephi 15:21).

He then advised the second group that He had still other
sheep He would visit, referring to the "lost" tribes (see 3
Nephi 16:1).

How many flocks and folds does the great Shepherd
have? We do not know.

Yet Jesus is so personal in His shepherding and tutoring!
Paul, while in a castle jail, was visited by the resurrected
Jesus. "And the night following the Lord stood by him, and
said, Be of good cheer, Paul: for as thou hast testified of me

in Jerusalem, so must thou bear witness also at Rome" (Acts 23:11).

Jesus' personalness is the more marvelous because it occurs in the midst of His universalness. Paul testified that God's Son "made the worlds" (Hebrews 1:2). Modern revelation confirms and amplifies: "And worlds without number have I created; and I also created them for mine own purpose; and by the Son I created them, which is mine Only Begotten" (Moses 1:33).

And the process is ongoing, for God's course is "one eternal round" (1 Nephi 10:19; D&C 3:2). "And as one earth shall pass away, and the heavens thereof even so shall another come; and there is no end to my works, neither to my words" (Moses 1:38).

Even so, Jesus knows and cares for each individual; He watches carefully over the seemingly smallest of things. He was especially and tenderly disclosing to a believing, solitary woman of Samaria: "The woman saith unto him, I know that Messias cometh, which is called Christ: when he is come, he will tell us all things. Jesus saith unto her, I that speak unto thee am he." (John 4:25–26.)

Enoch exclaimed over God's creations, "And were it possible that man could number the particles of the earth, yea, millions of earths like this, it would not be a beginning to the number of thy creations; and thy curtains are stretched out still" (Moses 7:30).

Notice, however, what reassured and assuaged Enoch most about Jesus amid His creations: "And *yet thou art there*, and thy bosom is there; and also thou art just; thou art merciful and kind forever" (Moses 7:30, emphasis added). Are not those the very same fundamental facts which you and I likewise find most crucial and most reassuring?

No wonder Paul wrote that in Christ "all things hold together" (Revised Standard Version, Colossians 1:15). All that really matters is held together by Jesus, who created the worlds. His merciful atonement rescues us all. His love encloses us all. Even when, in a particular time of life, things may seem to come apart for us individually, He holds "all things together." Thus Nephi, though perplexed, could declare: "I know that he loveth his children; nevertheless, I do not know the meaning of all things" (1 Nephi 11:17).

We likewise may not understand the meaning of all that is happening to us or around us, but we can actually know that God loves us personally!

To a suffering Joseph Smith, the resurrected Lord counseled tenderly and personally, "All these things shall give thee experience, and shall be for thy good" (D&C 122:7). The universal Lord put matters in further perspective by saying to Joseph that all these things would be "but a small moment" (D&C 121:7). He reassured imprisoned and lonely Joseph by providing this stunning perspective: "The ends of the earth shall inquire after thy name" (D&C 122:1).

Oh, the meekness and the majesty of Jesus!

Jesus was born in humble circumstances at Bethlehem under a special, heavenly sign. Yet on the Eastern hemisphere only a few shepherds and several wise men paid any heed to that sign. Herod worried. However, when Jesus comes to reign in majesty it will be different! There will be another sign, but this time "all people shall see it together" (D&C 88:93). Furthermore, we are told, "when the veil . . . which hideth the earth, shall be taken off, . . . all flesh shall see me together" (D&C 101:23).

What high drama! Jesus of Nazareth is our personal Savior and King. He is also the Lord of the universe. He is also the Lord of loving-kindness!

The Atonement is the chief expression of His loving-kindness. John Taylor explained Christ's special empathy:

Therefore it was necessary, when the Saviour was upon the earth, that he should be tempted in all points, like unto us, and "be touched with the feeling of our infirmities," to comprehend the weaknesses and strength, the perfections and imperfections of poor fallen human nature. And having accomplished the thing he came into the world to do; having had to grapple with the hypocrisy, corruption, weakness, and imbecility of man; having met with temptation and trial in all its various forms, and overcome, he has become a "faithful High Priest" to intercede for us in the everlasting kingdom of His Father. He knows how to estimate and put a proper value upon human nature, for he having been placed in the same position as we are, knows how to bear with our weaknesses and infirmities, and can fully comprehend the depth, power, and strength of the afflictions and trials that men have to cope with in this world, and thus understandingly and by experience, he can bear with them.[3]

Jesus' glorious but grim atonement fulfilled so many prophecies. In the process He was to be spat upon (1 Nephi 19:9); struck; scourged (Mosiah 3:9). He was to be offered vinegar and gall (Psalm 69:21). The very words of His agonizing soul-cry of aloneness were prophesied by David (Psalm 22:1). None of His bones was to be broken (Psalm 34:20).

Jesus performed what the Book of Mormon calls the "infinite atonement." Infinite, first, because the Son of God was sacrificed. No animal nor even ordinary mortal could have satisfied divine justice. Second, the Atonement was infinite in that it benefits all, "For as in Adam all die, even so in Christ shall all be made alive" (1 Corinthians 15:22). Third, infinite suffering was required of Him in order to bring to pass the infinite atonement.

So great were His burdens that when Jesus entered Gethsemane He "fell on the ground" (Mark 14:35). Matthew records that as Jesus "went a little further" into the Garden of Gethsemane, "he fell on his face, and prayed" (Matthew 26:39). He thus did not kneel down to pray primly or briefly. Later an unidentified angel appeared to strengthen Him in His agony (Luke 22:43).

Amid the awful suffering at Gethsemane, He was, wrote Mark, "sore amazed" and "very heavy" (Mark 14:33), meaning "astonished," "awestruck," "depressed," "dejected." It was so much worse than the keenest of intellects could have imagined! Then came His anguished "Abba cry," the cry of a child in distress for His Father: "And he said, Abba, Father, all things are possible unto thee; take away this cup from me: nevertheless not what I will, but what thou wilt" (Mark 14:36).

It was a real pleading followed by real submissiveness.

He who was sinless bore the sins of billions, from Adam to the end of the world, including those of even the "vilest of sinners" (Mosiah 28:4). As He ransomed us, Jesus experienced what He later described as "the fierceness of the wrath of the Almighty God" (D&C 76:107; 88:106). We should ponder that telling phrase, but we cannot begin to comprehend it!

In order to ransom us all, He passed through the experience of having "descended below all things, in that he comprehended all things" (D&C 88:6; see also 122:8). He was thereby confirmed and perfected in His marvelous empathy.

Several years ago, Christian physicians who wrote in the *Journal of American Medicine* indicated they felt that, because of the loss of blood when he was scourged, Jesus would have been in serious if not critical condition before He ever carried a portion of His cross to Calvary.[4] No wonder He needed help to carry it.

Scholars say He was likely scourged with a Roman flagellum, which would resemble a "cat-o'-nine-tails," with sharp, metallic objects at the end of each thong. If he assumed the usual posture for scourging, He would have been kneeling over before His scourger, thus the tensed muscles of the back would be more easily torn and shredded. He would have lost much blood in addition to what He lost earlier while bleeding at every pore in Gethsemane. Therefore, wrote these physicians, Jesus was in serious if not critical condition before Calvary.

Elder Talmage wrote that the Father "seems" to have withdrawn the support of His immediate Presence from Jesus while on the cross, so that Jesus' personal triumph would be complete.[5]

In commenting on the agony of the Atonement, Brigham Young went even further:

> God never bestows upon His people, or upon an individual, superior blessings without a severe trial to prove them . . . to see whether they will keep their covenants with Him. . . . For this express purpose the Father with-

drew His spirit from His Son, at the time he was to be crucified. Jesus had been with his Father, talked with Him, dwelt in His bosom, and knew all about heaven, about making the earth, about the transgression of man, and what would redeem the people, and that he was the character who was to redeem the sons of earth, and the earth itself from all sin that had come upon it. The light, knowledge, power, and glory with which he was clothed were far above, or exceeded that of all others who had been upon the earth after the fall, consequently at the very moment, at the hour when the crisis came for him to offer up his life, the Father withdrew Himself, withdrew His Spirit, and cast a veil over him. That is what made him sweat blood. If he had had the power of God upon him, he would not have sweat blood; but all was withdrawn from him, and a veil was cast over him, and he then plead with the Father not to forsake him.[6]

On the cross in the midst of the awful aloneness, there came, verbatim, the prophesied, soul-rending cry, "My God, my God, why hast thou forsaken me?" (Matthew 27:46; see also Psalm 22:1.)

Was that awful aloneness included in Alma's prophecy about Jesus' need to know certain things "according to the flesh"? Was it imposed in order for Jesus to experience what it is like to feel forsaken? (See Alma 7:11–12.) In any case, Jesus felt forsaken and alone. He could justifiably say, "none were with me" (D&C 133:50).

Both Nephi and Alma said Jesus would bear and thus know the pains and sicknesses of all men, women, and children (see Isaiah 53:4; 2 Nephi 9:21; Mosiah 14:4; Alma 7:11–12). The "infinite atonement" thus brought infinite understanding and infinite empathy.

We have no scriptures informing us of the Father's feelings as He watched His Son suffer. But He was a perfect Father with perfect empathy!

In His retrospective comments on the awful Atonement, Jesus tells us that He "suffered both body and spirit," experiencing incredibly interactive pain (see D&C 19:18–19).

Those comments do not even mention His having been spat upon, struck, scourged, given vinegar and gall, and so forth. He does say, however, that He trembled because of pain and "would that [he] might not shrink"—that is, by failing to partake fully of the bitter cup and thereby finishing the Atonement. To shrink means to "recoil," "pull back," "cower"! Mercifully for all of us, Jesus did not shrink!

Instead He drained the bitter cup; did so without becoming bitter and did so without losing His marvelous meekness amid His great victory! "Nevertheless, glory be to the Father, and I partook and finished my preparations unto the children of men" (D&C 19:19). Premortally He promised to give all the glory to the Father (see Moses 4:2). Postmortally He did just that (see D&C 19:19).

How could He accomplish the Atonement?" Abinadi said, because He let His own will be totally "swallowed up in the will of the Father" (Mosiah 15:7).

Jesus had been totally submissive "from the beginning." "I have drunk out of that bitter cup which the Father hath given me, and have glorified the Father in taking upon me the sins of the world, in the which I have suffered the will of the Father in all things from the beginning" (3 Nephi 11:11).

Why did He do it? He did not have to die! He could have pulled back!

"And the world, because of their iniquity, shall judge him to be a thing of naught; wherefore they scourge him, and he suffereth it; and they smite him, and he suffereth it. Yea, they spit upon him, and he suffereth it, because of his *loving kindness* and his *long-suffering* towards the children of men." (1 Nephi 19:9, emphasis added.) Note the focus on His supernal qualities of "loving-kindness" and "longsuffering."

When He comes again, unlike His coming to the signifying meekness of the manger, He will come in overwhelming majesty and power. In at least one appearance He will come in red apparel to remind us that He shed His blood for us (see D&C 133:48; Isaiah 63:1). Among the astounding accompanying events, stars will fall from the heavens, as Christ will declare, "I have trodden the winepress alone . . . and none were with me" (D&C 133:50).

What will we and those who witness these marvelous events speak of, then and later? Not the solar display with falling stars! Instead, we will speak of Jesus' "loving-kindness." For how long will we so exclaim? "Forever and ever" (D&C 133:52). The more we come to know of Jesus and the Atonement, the more we shall praise and adore Him "forever and ever."

Meanwhile, however, He has asked us to become more like Him in attributes and qualities. We cannot be "valiant in the testimony of Jesus" (D&C 76:79) unless we really strive to become more like Him.

Brigham Young described the consecration that will be needed: "When the will, passions, and feelings of a person are perfectly submissive to God and His requirements, that person is sanctified. It is for my will to be swallowed up in the will of God, that will lead me into all good, and crown me ultimately with immortality and eternal lives."[7]

What consecration of conduct! How crucial such submission is! As Erastus Snow observed: "The Father withholds his Spirit from us in proportion as we desire the gratification of our own will. We interpose a barrier between us and our Father, that he cannot, consistently with himself, move upon us so as to control our actions."[8]

As we pray over the sacrament, do we not plead to have His Spirit "always" with us?

For those whose wills truly become swallowed up in the will of God, the resplendent rendezvous spoken of by the prophet Mormon (who, by the way, knew whereof he spoke) will one day be a personal reality. Mormon declares that Jesus waits "with open arms" to receive the repentant and fully faithful. They will one day be "clasped in the arms of Jesus"! (Mormon 6:17; 5:11.)

May we so live *now* in order to be so welcomed *then*—by
the Lord of loving-kindness and of the far-flung vineyard!

Much love,
Grandfather

Notes

1. *Teachings*, p. 216.
2. *JD* 7:275.
3. *JD* 1:148.
4. William D. Edwards, et al., "On the Physical Death of Jesus Christ," *Journal of the American Medical Association*, 21 March 1986, p. 1455.
5. See James E. Talmage, *Jesus the Christ* (Salt Lake City: Deseret Book Company, 1962), p. 661.
6. *JD* 3:205–6.
7. *JD* 2:123. See also Mosiah 15:7.
8. *JD* 7:352.

Scripture Index

OLD TESTAMENT

NEW TESTAMENT

BOOK OF MORMON

DOCTRINE AND COVENANTS

PEARL OF GREAT PRICE

Subject Index

— A —

Abilities, converging with integrity, 146–47
  in relation to opportunities, 143–47
Abuse, consequence of pornography, 99
  verbal, 150
  worked against in good causes, 85
  See also Drug abuse
Acceptance, of God's schedule, 84
Accountability, mixed with mercy attests God's justice, 27
Acknowledgment, of gifts given by God, 123
  of God, 26
  of God's timetable, 27
  of small blessings, 30
Activities, fleeting and enduring satisfactions from, 72
Adam and Eve, instructed to dress the earth, 75
Adoration, of Jesus Christ, 203
Adversity, an experience of life, 128
  helps spiritual purification, 114
  teaches empathy, 107
Affection, a gift of God, 66
Afflictions, borne better than small slights, 55
  experienced by Jesus Christ, 3
  seen as blessings, 14, 107
  See also Trials
Agency. *See* moral agency
Agony, awaits when agency goes wrong, 85
  of Christ in Gethsemane, 207
AIDS, 83
Alcohol, ruins the future, 76
Angel, strengthened Christ in His agony, 207
Answers, to "why" questions, 156
Apostles, have divine authority, 79
  must delegate the small causes, 90
Apostleship, 88–90
  sacred and special calling, 89
  authority to bear testimony of Jesus Christ, 125
Application, of correct principles, 138
Appreciation, expressed genuinely, 55
  for good people, 104
Associations, in the spirit world, 93
Atonement, 61, 169
  awful and agonizing, 1
  benefits all, 205, 207

brings infinite understanding and empathy, 209
chief expression of the Savior's love, 206
Christ's feelings during, 1
fulfilled many prophecies, 207
greatest gift, 202
praised forever, 106
required infinite suffering, 207
the sacrifice of the Son of God, 207
voluntary, 1
Attention, becomes a form of validation, 55
Attitudes, hard to let go of, 119
Attributes, required of the truly faithful, 152
Authority, divinely resting in priesthood keys, 79
  given to Apostles to testify of Jesus Christ, 125
  operates with democracy, 16

— B —

Behavior, places some outside of happiness, 169
Belief, grows into confirmed faith, 102
  in angels, 174
  in God, 174
  in personal immortality, 175
  in prophets, 174
  step to acquiring spiritual knowledge, 101–2
Blessings, acknowledging God's hand in, 30
  come by obedience to God's laws, 73
  given by Jesus, 3
  given if we keep our covenants, 159
  of the Book of Mormon, 49
  of the Light of Christ, 29–30
  patriarchal, 159
  preceded by difficulties, 4
  predicated on obedience, 179
  tied to our obedience, 198
  to be remembered, 109–11
  wrongly regarded as "givens," 110
Blood, sweat during the Atonement, 2
Book of Life, 55
Book of Mormon, testimony of its authenticity, 164
  truth from the earth, 49
Bread of Life, always gives enough and to spare, 198

— M —

Majesty, of Jesus Christ, 206, 210, 141
Man, possesses germs of God-like attributes, 21
Mankind, free to choose, 85
Meekness, 160
  balanced with judgment, 138
  determined by capacity to love, 21
  helps us meet challenges, 23
  in remembering origin of gifts, 123
  in teaching, 43
  inherent in the Mortal Messiah, 202
  learned from frustrations, 176
  necessary to learn spiritual lessons, 173
  needed to speak at the right time, 132
  needs to be constant, 108
  not dependent on the praise of men, 135
  of Jesus Christ, 206
  overcomes the natural man, 118
  product of gratitude to God, 31
Memories, enhanced with the passage of time, 200
  lacking in second estate, 10
  nourish in the years ahead, 201
  of premortality, 170, 200, 201
  provoked by the word of God, 182
Men and women of Christ, easily entreated, 89
Men, lifted up to God through Jesus Christ, 26
Mercy, balanced with justice, 138
  extended in families, 12
  meets agency, 191
  mixed with moral agency, 27
  of God in the spirit world, 94
  of God unchallengeable, 55
  openly acknowledged, 34, 82, 169
  overpowers justice, 66
Millennium, denominational differences existing during, 142
Minds, to yield to the gospel, 101
Misery, cannot hold joy hostage, 169
  reduced in families, 157
Missionaries, should have clean hands and pure hearts, 36
Mistakes, can be repented for, 146
  should not immobilize us, 137–38
Modesty, a balance between pride and prostration, 138
  a part of faith, 136
  helps us to be patient in life, 136
Money, traded for time, 53
Moral agency, 28–29, 198
  constantly abused, 81

exercised by doubters, 191
expected without human misery, 68
given by God, 81
honored by Jesus Christ, 148
in relation to suffering, 81–85
irrevocably related to eternal joy, 66
mixed with mercy attests God's justice, 27
requires the existence of alternatives, 37
uncompromised by God's foreknowledge, 26
usage a personal determination, 65
Mortality, structured for trials, 108
Moses, heard every great matter, 90
Mourning, added to suffering brings wisdom, 173
Murmuring, because of difficulties, 3
Mussolini, took away freedoms, 146
Mysteries, revealed from God in confidence, 70

— N —

Narrow passages, navigated by strict obedience, 13
Natural man, 118
  enemy to God and His children, 196
  complains about the darkness, 174
  consumed in selfishness, 12
  finds praying difficult, 178
  heavy to carry, 18
  must be put off, 18–19
  resists spiritual learning, 106
  to be put off with longsuffering, 15
  to be put off with open eyes and hearts, 119
  welcomes temptations, 151
Needs, placed before God in prayer, 179
Nephi, asked why, 95
Nourishment, of the spirit, 121
Nurturing, within the Church, 80

— O —

Obedience, a true friend of intelligence, 102
  brings generous blessings, 73
  develops character, 102
  in gaining intelligence, 37
  leads to more knowledge, 102–3
  symbiotic with longsuffering, 13
  to the Lord's will, 127
Offenders, dealing with, 161–62
Omniscience, of God fragmented by some, 61